THE POUCHPLAN BUDGET

THE POUCHPLAN BUDGET

The Simple Way to Find Hidden Money, Improve Your Life, and Build Wealth

MITCHELL WALKER

Straight Path Books, Publisher

Straight Path Books, 1110 South Cesar Chavez Blvd., #1106, Dallas, TX 75201

Library of Congress Control Number: 2017909773

ISBN-13: 978-0-9991335-0-7

For bulk copy purchases, or other questions, please visit www.PouchPlan.com

Cover and Interior Design by AuthorSupport.com

Author Photograph by Shaney Daniels

Printed in the United States of America

I am delighted to dedicate this book to
my wife, Suzanne Walker.

Without you by my side this book and
so many other dreams of mine would
still be just that, dreams.

FOREWORD

One of the more important subjects is how somebody chooses to handle their money. Every choice made about money will have positive or negative consequences and will affect many areas of your life. Mitchell likes to say "If you do money right, life gets easier and better. You do it wrong, it only get's harder." I know from years of my own experience that this is a true statement.

My professional career has been focused around manufacturing. To be successful in manufacturing you need systems which deliver expected results, can be consistently repeated, and can be measured for success. It is not much of a leap in our thought process to consider you are manufacturing your future with each financial choice you make. A system which provides these elements may be just the tool to produce the financial life one desires. I see all of these in the PouchPlan.

I also see a lot of "Marmon" in the PouchPlan. Mitchell was the Vice President of Finance for our sister company, Dekoron Wire & Cable for 14 years. I see USa in his separating expenses into two "piles" and then automating a checking account to pay the "regular" ones. I see Kanbans established as cash is put into different sections of a pouch. I see 80/20 as he describes "have to", "need to", and "want to" types of expenses and how you set up a hierarchy to meet your dreams. And I see Lean as I consider an overall system that requires no accounting, bookkeeping, receipt posting, or even any math to produce an accurate and up to date budget in the hands of the user.

There is no doubt that many Americans struggle with financial literacy. The subject has not been a priority for our educational system and unless you were fortunate enough to pick up some good habits from parents or other sources, you may have felt like the deck was stacked against you. I am extremely happy to be providing this book to our employees to help address this issue. Please invest a couple of hours in yourself to read and then put into place the advice in *The PouchPlan Budget.* I think you will be glad you did. As a matter of fact, Mitchell calls it going from "Ouch to Pouch" and invites you to join him.

Gary Gagnon
President - RSCC Wire & Cable LLC

Table of Contents

PREFACE

Let's face it. How you handle money affects your mental and physical health, relationships, and self-esteem—basically, everything that contributes to your overall happiness. When you get your finances right, life gets easier, much easier. You get them wrong and life can become dreary and dreadful as you face a seemingly unending string of hurts and disappointments. The PouchPlan is a simple and easy-to-follow budget system that makes life easier. By the time you complete this book, you will be able to take control of your money—probably the most influential aspect of your life.

If you build a solid foundation, then it will be strong enough to support anything you want to build on top of it. However, if you build on a weak or shaky foundation, it is sure to fall. It does not matter if you are erecting a building, a business, a marriage, or a family, you must have a strong foundation to succeed. As is written in some great literature, "The wise man built his house upon a rock." You should aspire to be that wise individual.

The foundation of your financial life is a budget or plan. I have prepared, reviewed, and analyzed thousands of budgets during my fifteen years as a vice president of finance for a Berkshire Hathaway company. I have been fortunate to learn skills and techniques that are among the best practices available in corporate America. I have also learned from assisting hundreds of small businesses as a partner in a tax and bookkeeping business with multiple locations for eleven years. But I've seen things from the other end as well.

In the late 1980s, I went through a divorce and sold my struggling business, leaving me $100,000 in debt and unemployed. I still vividly remember looking for change under the couch cushions for gas money to take my seventh-grade daughter to volleyball practice. When you suffer a financial collapse, the collateral damage is extensive and extremely painful to those you love. The goal of this book is to prevent you from living a life in the rubble of poor financial choices. If you currently find yourself buried in the consequences of your past choices, the PouchPlan is your shovel to dig yourself out. If you are young and have never experienced this struggle, but you can feel the wobble as life's storms pass by, the PouchPlan is a solid foundation on which you can build your financial structure.

Once you've established a solid foundation, do you stop? Absolutely not! A foundation needs to be built upon, and a great one is out of sight and out of mind. No one wants to live in a basement or on a concrete slab for his or her whole life. Whether you prefer a two-story colonial or a minimalistic modern structure, you need a foundation to hold it up. I am here to provide you with a foundation that can incorporate many different types of financial "additions." Just like you add carpet, tile, and plumbing to a home, there are many supplements to your financial base. But you need to have the foundation in place before you contemplate the add-ons.

The PouchPlan is very personal to me. First, it was the shovel that I used to dig my family out of financial distress. Then, it served as the concrete from which I was able to construct a secure foundation. In 1993, I married the most remarkable woman, and we brought together a blended family of five children. We had an abundance of love and laughter, but, unfortunately, those things don't pay for groceries or dance lessons. In order to manage the financial needs of our family of seven, we combined ideas from many sources and mixed in some real-life experiences until we developed a simple-to-use and easy-to-maintain plan.

We have followed this plan with real blood, sweat, and tears for the last twenty-five years. I can assure you it stopped the financial bleeding, changed the source of sweat from stress to exercise, and turned tears of pain to tears of joy as we celebrated five college graduations, four weddings, and ten grandchildren (so far). The PouchPlan has been a faithful and trusted friend and source of freedom that we enjoy sharing with others.

If you will invest a few hours reading this book and putting the PouchPlan into place, the results in your life will be amazing. I mentioned earlier the power of money and how it exponentially increases the impact of whatever it comes in contact with. Author Matthew

Bennett calls money the "magic multiplier." This is not a declaration of the morality or immorality of money, but just its amazing ability. The PouchPlan is going to help you harness that power over your personal finances. Let it do the heavy lifting as you build a great financial future on a solid and secure foundation.

The PouchPlan uses the power of a plan to simplify and reduce financial chaos in your life. The result will leave you with peace of mind. You will be free from fear, struggle, and doubt. It is amazing how many areas of our lives are impacted by our financial situation and how freeing it is to not have these areas burdened by financial worry.

In order for any plan to work, it must be *doable.* Think about this for a moment. We have millions of fat, broke Americans. Do you really think they are fat and broke because they want to be? Do you think they got up one morning and said, "I think I will set up a plan to become fat and broke"? I can promise you the vast majority of these people are not happy with their situations and would love to change them. Most diets and budgets fail because they simply are not doable by those who need them the most. A diet that requires hard-to-find ingredients, extra preparation time, and special cooking skills is going to fail for most people.

I've seen the same shortcomings with many personal budgets. A budget that requires constant maintenance to be up-to-date, a degree in accounting to keep accurately, or is difficult to adjust to life's constant surprises is going to be dropped very quickly. My family's real-life experiences have honed the PouchPlan to a manageable level of time requirement (less than fifteen minutes per month on average) and effort (moving actual cash a couple of centimeters) while also providing a simple and easy way to react no matter what life sends your way (again, moving actual cash a couple of centimeters). The number one reason people fall off the PouchPlan is that the plan improves their financial situation so much that they think they don't need it anymore. We even fell for that one once!

This book is divided into three parts. Part 1 is a big-picture overview of why and how the PouchPlan works. Part 2 describes what I have found to be the necessary ingredients for putting a plan together and making it a success. Here, you will read about the conceptual view of the PouchPlan as well as motivational stories shared by other PouchPlan users. Part 3 is the "let's roll up our sleeves and get this done" section. Here you will find line-by-line instructions and specific options that can be used to handle the unique situations in your financial life. I can't say I've seen every imaginable circumstance, but I've been personally and professionally exposed to many more than most people. I have put together dozens of the best tips and tactics that can help guide you as you create your own plan.

The PouchPlan will give you the power to change your financial future very quickly. I am giving you a tool that delivers strong, proven, solid, and repeatable actions to lead you in your efforts. Its simplicity may surprise you at times. (Please be aware that "simplicity" does not mean "weakness.")

You have now been formally introduced to the PouchPlan. Of course, the real fun in any relationship is getting to know each other better. Jump on in; there is nothing holding you back.

Oh, yes; a few declarations. The names used in the examples in the book are made up. Please don't go looking for your ex thinking he or she finally got his or her financial act together and you are going to get what you're owed. I don't want you to be disappointed if your former partner hasn't yet discovered the PouchPlan. Also, for several reasons, I have occasionally combined the individual actions of several PouchPlan users under a single fictitious name. But all the laughing and crying moments you read about are real.

On my website, www.PouchPlan.com, you can download the spreadsheet for free and get the latest FAQs and read my blog. I would like to hear what you like or don't like about the PouchPlan and any other comments, positive or negative, you might have. If the PouchPlan does not help you, I've failed in my mission. If you can share with me where you struggle, perhaps I can make changes or additions that fix the issue(s), and you will be able to reap all the benefits available from the system. The odds are that if you struggle with a situation, others do as well. You could possibly help hundreds of other people besides yourself if you will reach out to me. My best and current contact information is listed on the website under the "Contact Us" link.

Cordially,
Mitchell Walker

PART 1

The Big Picture

I promise you I will not waste your time, effort, money and hope on something that doesn't work. Part 1 of this book is the view from the top on why and how the PouchPlan will work for you. I will share with you how and when many features of the plan were developed in the messiness of real life. I will share with you how the plan was revised and improved to reduce that messiness and the results of those efforts. I will also give you a high-level view of the plan so you can see how the three main parts fit effortlessly together.

As you read Part 1, you will begin to get a sense of why the PouchPlan doubles or triples the success rate of other types of budgeting plans. You will see in the examples how very ordinary people with no expertise in accounting or math can follow the plan for years. People often ask me if the PouchPlan will work for everyone. I tell them of course not. If you do not know how to spend money, it will not work for you. For the rest of you, it will.

CHAPTER 1

Why Does the PouchPlan Work?

The PouchPlan works because it is simple. It mirrors your life rather than forcing you to fit your budgeting into someone else's vision or plan. It works because it gives you instructions paycheck by paycheck. It works because it is based on sound budgeting principals and comes with specific and easy- to-follow directions. It works because it is a marriage of professional knowledge blended with twenty-five years of actual use in a family of seven.

If you can do these three things, you can do the PouchPlan:

1. Write down your income paycheck by paycheck.
2. Write down your expenses that do not vary in amount or date each month.

3. Write down your expenses that vary in amount and date each month.

The PouchPlan will do the rest. The spreadsheet that is referenced in the book is available for free at my website, www.PouchPlan.com. With this information, the PouchPlan budget system will provide specific instructions for you to follow on each and every payday.

THE "OH, NO" MOMENT

We were semi newlyweds of about six months when the cracks started to form in our handling of our monthly bills and expenses. My wife, Suzanne, was working part-time as the billing clerk for a law firm, which required her to travel and be away from home a couple of nights per month. I was a salesperson at a local car dealership. As this was a second marriage for both of us, we had a blended family. I contributed a seventeen-year-old son and a fourteen-year-old daughter, and Suzanne had two daughters, ages nine and five, and a son aged seven. Most people would probably agree the odds were stacked against us from the beginning. Financial struggles could definitely sink us if we did not get our act together.

We (six of us) needed to make a two-hour trip back to the Dallas area one weekend, and the dealership I worked for let us use a Suburban that was recently traded in. Suzanne had originally resisted the idea of taking a Suburban because she thought they were huge, ugly, and impossible to park. We put the youngest two in the far back seat and the oldest two in the row behind us. After about thirty minutes of blissful quiet (of course, the fourteen-year-old wasn't talking to anyone in the family by now, anyway), my wife leaned over and gave me a peck on the cheek and said something to the effect, "This is wonderful; you may never get me out of one of these."

We decided to buy the Suburban, but my mediocre credit resulted in a high interest rate from the bank. Suzanne was talking to her parents on the phone shortly afterward, and her father offered to finance the vehicle at about a 30 percent lower rate than what the bank had quoted. Apparently, this was not an uncommon practice for him as he had previously financed some of his other children's endeavors. I was a bit uncomfortable with the offer, but the much better rate was a no-brainer. Our only other debt was our house and an old bank note of mine. But, with a household of seven and a bunch of monthly living expenses and bills, it did not take long for the chaos to surface.

About the third or fourth month after we had bought the Suburban, we (and by *we*, I mean ***I***) forgot about the payment and sent it to my father-in-law about five days late. I did not hear about it at the time, but apparently my wife did. Early the next month, I received a kind, but firm, lecture from my wife. She reminded me that the loan came from her parents' retirement money, and they depended on us paying it back—and paying it back on time.

Dadgummit, I do not know what it is about my brain, but sometimes the more I concentrate on something, the more likely I am to forget it. Fast forward a couple weeks, and unfortunately, I realized I had made the same mistake again.

But, it gets worse than just being a late payment. I go to write the check and realize that I do not have enough money in my account to cover it. I'm going to have to tell Suzanne I forgot again and ask to move some money from her account into mine. What man wants to go tell his wife of less than a year he is a nincompoop and needs money? I, of course, had been only looking at events from my sad, suffering point of view. My wife calls to let her folks know we are sending the check, and her mom tells her that her dad has been so distraught that he can barely speak about it. Each day the check did not arrive, he got worse.

This incident provided the motivation to put into place what would become the PouchPlan. I have been blessed with an amazing wife, but talking about money is not easy for her. But she managed to push through, and we set up a budget based on an envelope system of dividing our cash for our expenses. While talking about money may be low on her list of things she likes, her administration skills are absolutely off the charts! In no time, she threw away the envelopes and replaced them with a coupon-sized expandable folder with each divider labeled for an expense category. She told me that if I could give her instructions detailing how much and when to put money into each section of the folder, it would take a lot of stress off her. I immediately began to develop a spreadsheet that would provide her with the information she needed.

While my wife's strengths are organization and administration, mine are numbers and big-picture systems. She really can heard cats while for some reason I can't remember your name. I will recall your age, phone number, date of birth, weight, or any other number you share with me. So, I started to put together a spreadsheet that would take the budget numbers and link them to the time of the month the expenses were due. This was also about the time that electronic bill payment was becoming more widely offered. I did not like the idea of either of us carrying around a lot of cash, so I decided to use "outsourcing" for as many expenses as possible to reduce that exposure.

Very quickly, we knew we were moving in a direction that made the envelope budget process much simpler and safer. A new type of thinking, one that intuitively made sense based on how regular an expense was in amount and frequency, was beginning to take shape. These types of expenses seemed to make up the majority of funds expended each month as well. The question we asked ourselves was, "What if we put the money for those regular expenses in one 'envelope' called the 'bank account' and allowed them to be paid automatically?" We decided to give that a try and see what happened.

We identified all the regular expenses as defined above and left enough money from each paycheck in our account to pay those as they came due. Using the bank account as the "outsourced payment" category reduced the cash we handled by more than half. Actually, the maximum amount ever held on hand was reduced by far more than half, reducing the risk associated with carrying cash. It also reduced the number of pouch categories to a more manageable number. Outsourcing as many bills as possible to automatic payments has a major impact on simplifying your budget.

The simpler your budget, the better chance you have of using it successfully. (I will share much more on this and other topics in the "Tips and Techniques" section in part 3 of the book.)

Good fortune had smiled upon us. We had been able to do away with the three biggest problems of the traditional envelope system: First, the amount of cash exposure was extremely reduced; second, the number of envelopes requiring funding and tracking were cut dramatically; and third, the hassle of trying to pay bills with cash was totally gone. There were a couple of other very pleasant side effects as well. My personal favorites are balancing a bank account with no outstanding checks and not having to *remember* to pay any bill.

IMPROVING AS WE LEARN

If we had stopped right there, I believe we would have had a budget plan system that we could have implemented and depended on. But my wife's cat-herding ability said, "Not so fast. We still have a bunch of irregular expenses, and you promised me detailed directions on how to handle them." The definition we came up with for an irregular expense is very simple: *Irregular expenses* vary in amount and/or frequency in their occurrence. I tend to learn a lot from examples, so let me give you examples of each.

Some common *regular expenses* are items such as your house payment or rent; car payments; bank and student loans; car, life, and house insurance; child care; cell phones; cable TV; and probably most utilities. Once again, regular expenses in the PouchPlan are due in the same amount and the same time of each month. *Irregular expenses* are items such as food, clothes, household items, entertainment, gifts, dry cleaning, car repairs, gasoline and transportation, and miscellaneous. Irregular expenses vary in timing and amount, sometimes wildly, during a month. Thinking about your expenses in this way provides a framework that matches your actual living activities. The PouchPlan takes what most people are already doing in their spending habits and uses this familiarity to make setting up and following a plan seem natural and normal.

Of course, we hit some speed bumps with our early attempts. The irregular expenses were most often the cause of the slowdowns. After deciding on several main categories, I pretty quickly asked my wife how much we spent on each of those categories. The answer I received was, "How much do I have to spend?" I will tell you that we are going on our twenty-fifth year of marriage, and we have never even had a heated discussion regarding money, much less an argument. I give a whole bunch of credit to the PouchPlan for that achievement. A powerful result of a plan, especially the PouchPlan, is you have a guide that helps move you together to an agreed-upon destination. The PouchPlan does not take sides; it is already on both sides.

It was still necessary that we settle on amounts for these irregular expenses, so we agreed to "guesstimate." This was way scarier for my wife than me, as she was the one who would be handling the expenditures of our household and day-to-day expenses. The solution we landed on helped overcome some of her concerns, and I now recommend it for everyone. We established an oversized "Miscellaneous" category, and we agreed to consider the other amounts as temporary and subject to change. Now, we were able to determine the temporary amounts for each irregular expense category.

One of the first things you will notice about the PouchPlan is that I give you specific instructions for each and every paycheck. This is a powerful tool that frees you up to live your plan rather than always having to work on it. I went to work on the spreadsheet to have it automatically calculate the cash available from each paycheck after depositing the amount needed to pay the regular expenses into the bank. The money left over from the paycheck after paying the regular expenses was withdrawn to fund the pouch's irregular expenses. This takes on average less than five minutes to complete.

I now needed to set up instructions that would tell us how much to fund each irregular expense category per paycheck. The choice of when and how much to fund each pouch category was a combination of simple need and common sense. We had to eat and we had to have toilet paper. Those two needs got enough funds to carry through to the next paycheck and maybe just a little bit more. We also had to have some gas money, but entertainment, haircuts, and dry cleaning could all be partially funded or moved to another pay period or paycheck. A strength of the envelope system and the PouchPlan is its flexibility to move money around to cover the normal ebb and flow of life's financial tides. This flexibility gives you more room to handle changes and to safely stay within the overall boundaries you have established.

Within just a few months, we had a much better idea of what our irregular expenses required and made those adjustments with ease. Over that period of time, I had the chance to link the funds available from each paycheck to the pouch's requirements on the spreadsheet. The spreadsheet was now a one-time, fill-in-the-blank activity that stipulated the exact amount of cash to be placed in each category of the pouch from each paycheck. Open those barn doors; the kitties are coming in!

I left you hanging about the story of the Suburban and my father-in-law. I do not want you to get the wrong idea about this very good man. Even though we met the monthly due date precisely over the next two months, he determined it was not worth worrying about and decided to give us the vehicle. Yes, he GAVE it to us.

I am sharing these stories with you because I want you to know why the PouchPlan works. This is not some pie-in-the-sky, theoretical experiment. The PouchPlan was originated and improved upon in the messiness of the real life of a blended family of seven. It has had to handle everything from auto repairs to vet bills, from steady paychecks to commission income. It showed us the way to take care of five college degrees and three daughters' weddings. Along the way, we've moved from a household of seven to empty nesters. The PouchPlan has been the bedrock financial tool we have depended on no matter the situation. We laugh about it now, but for years the common reply to "Can I have…" was "Talk to the Pouch."

As I mentioned earlier, I also know a thing or two about budgets, professionally speaking. I've spent the last fifteen years as the vice president of finance for an international manufacturing entity owned by Berkshire Hathaway. Prior to this position, I spent eleven years assisting small businesses with their accounting and tax needs as a partner of a bookkeeping and tax preparation service. I've also owned or been a partner in five other businesses of which I was responsible for the financial areas. I've even taken on a one-year term as interim chief financial officer (CFO) for a college and have served as a county commissioner and city councilman in my local community. I have seen and prepared thousands of budgets.

Businesses and governments have major advantages when it comes to budgeting. They can throw tremendous amounts of resources at the preparation, upkeep, and reporting of budgets. But they have their weaknesses, too. Many budgets of these entities are prepared and reviewed by people who are far away from the actual drivers of the income and expenses. My experience has taught me that the further you are from a problem, the less likely you are to contribute to its solution.

All too often, corporate managements have used budgets as a way of gaining compliance and power rather than earning those through performance and leadership. Many a poor manager has relied on underperformance against a budget as a reason to discipline or discharge employees who had little control over the situation they faced. Government abuses of budgeting are legendary and mindboggling. When someone uses a tool incorrectly, bad things typically happen. The more powerful the tool, the greater the potential for good or for damage.

Individuals and families are typically limited in time, finances, and expertise when it comes to budgeting. The good news is that they have the advantages of personal knowledge of their objectives, real-time feedback of the budget's effectiveness, the ability to make adjustments instantly, and most importantly, skin in the game. The PouchPlan works so well because it eradicates these disadvantages while leaving all the advantages. It requires very little time each month and literally no ongoing expense. The spreadsheet's fill-in-the-blank format reduces the expertise required as it automatically links and calculates your required actions. The *PouchPlan* book provides the remaining knowledge necessary with both high-level principles and specific instructions.

LIFE GETS EASIER

I would love to claim that I was so smart that I set out to accomplish all these great objectives when I put together the first spreadsheet. Alas, it is not so. Every benefit was the result of learning from the shortfalls or failures during actual use. Twenty-plus years of real-life pressure has produced a system that can be followed by anyone to lay the cornerstone building block to financial improvement—a usable and doable plan. It has worked for us, it has worked for others, and it will work for you.

The picture I've painted of myself up to this point is a bit incomplete and may make you uneasy without hearing the rest. Prior to my marriage to Suzanne, I went through an unexpected divorce and had a struggling business that I ending up selling for pennies on the dollar just to get out. When the dust settled, there was no job, and I was thousands of dollars in debt. When the fog of failure descends on your life, it can be debilitating. I've been to the bottom before, and the view from there is awful. But the best way out and up is to start stacking good decision on top of good decision. Pretty soon, you can see the top of the hole. Then the hole's horizon disappears and a new horizon comes into view. This one is large and growing. So is your spirit.

I'm not going to insult your intelligence and tell you that the PouchPlan solved all these problems. But I will tell you that my financial choices and actions played a big part. As a matter of fact, a friend of mine who was a district judge in Texas told me that financial issues were a factor in eight out of ten divorces that came through his court. Think about that statement for just a second. The relationship that has been foundational to societies for millenniums, marriage, is wounded by financial problems more than any other issue.

This demonstrates the power money plays in our lives. This statistic literally shouts that for a marriage to flourish, you must have this area under control and in agreement. Financial ignorance can kill a marriage. I mentioned that my wife and I have never even had a heated discussion regarding money in over twenty years. That does not mean we did not discuss money; it means that when we did, it was within the framework of how to adjust the Pouch to accommodate this new need or that new challenge. Over the hundreds of times we've had to make adjustments, we were always able to come out of the process feeling good about our decisions and about each other.

Once the money decisions move to the positive side of the equation in your life or relationships, you will benefit from the exponentially powerful characteristic of money and receive rewards you did not expect. We had a stay-at-home mom describe to us the impact on her as she divided up her cash into their family's pouch one afternoon.

"I realized as I put money in the sections labeled 'Kids' Activities,' 'School,' 'Hair,' and 'Gifts' that I was distributing my husband's efforts to others. My eyes teared up, and I thought what an unselfish man I have married. I felt very lucky and very loved."

The PouchPlan contributes so much because it directs this powerful tool called money to take care of the areas of life you decide are the most valuable. I call it moving from "ouch" to "pouch."

As I close this chapter, I want you to know that the PouchPlan will help you to achieve a greater degree of financial success. The level of your income, the amount of your net worth, your age, your education, or the lack of any of these factors does not matter. The concepts and principles have proven themselves over and over again in all situations. The PouchPlan is doable and usable by all. Handle your money right, and life gets easier; handle money wrong, and life gets harder. It's really as simple as that.

CHAPTER 2

How Does the PouchPlan Work?

The four things you must provide the PouchPlan with are the following:

1. Your income paycheck by paycheck
2. Your expenses that are the same in amount and date each month (*regular expenses*)
3. Your expenses that are *not* the same in amount or date each month (*irregular expenses*)
4. The date when these activities take place in the month (timing)

With this very basic information, the PouchPlan produces your monthly budget. This is where most budgeting plans stop. The problem with this strategy is that dumping all income and expenses into one basket for the month will leave dangerous gaps between when your money comes in and when it needs to go out. These gaps can cause late payments and bank overdrafts resulting in stress, embarrassment, and less money available for your living expenses. The PouchPlan is going to totally stop all late fees and overdraft charges from ever taking another dime from you and your family. Again, the PouchPlan spreadsheet is available for free download at my website, www.PouchPlan.com.

STEP 1: INCOME

I'm going to describe the simple steps that are required to make the system work. I will start with step 1 from the above list, your income. You enter your paycheck amount (either gross or take home; we will talk about the advantages of each later in the book) onto the spreadsheet. Next, you pick how often you are paid from a drop-down box that has weekly, biweekly, semimonthly, and monthly options. The PouchPlan spreadsheet automatically converts your individual paycheck into a monthly amount of income. Your monthly income can now be compared to your monthly expenses. Because you provided the pay periods, the system can match up the timing of your money coming in and the timing of your money going out.

You may have questions regarding income that does not come to you in the form of a paycheck or at regular amounts or times. That is OK and expected at this point. I'm asking you to give me a bit of trust right now. This chapter describes "how" the plan works looking down from a mile-high view. In the third part of the book, we will dig down into the weeds and look at how to handle many different situations. Your understanding of the concepts and principles of the PouchPlan will help you handle these different situations. My goal in this chapter is to lay out the concepts behind the plan so the instructions hang on a framework that is very clear and makes sense to you. So, I'm asking you to set aside specific concerns about how to handle varying income(s) and move forward believing you will be able to solve that question with my help.

STEP 2: REGULAR EXPENSES

Now on to step 2, your expenses that are the same amount each month and that will be paid at the same time each month. Your "regular" expenses should begin with all the legal commitments you have made. Your mortgage, rent, and any type of loans are listed in the regular expense section of the spreadsheet. Next, look at what bills come in every month. If you have a bank account, you can use a couple of months' statements as a guide. Utilities, cell phone, cable TV, internet, car and house insurance, dues, subscriptions, and life insurance are very common monthly bills. If you attend a church or place of worship, your donations should be set up under this area as well. Think about and look for any expenses that occur regularly even if they are paid more often than once per month. For example, many child-care facilities have payments due on the first and fifteenth of the month.

You are next going to tell the PouchPlan spreadsheet when each regular expense is paid. This is very simple on the PouchPlan. On the same line you entered the description and amount of each regular expense, you will now enter which week of the month the expense is to be paid. Your options are weeks 1, 2, 3, or 4 and are listed in separate columns. You simply record the same dollar amount in the proper weekly column as you entered next to the description. I have also included the days of the month covered by each weekly period to help you. For example, week 1 covers days 1–7, week 2 days 8-15, and so on. I've also included an "Off By" column that lets you know whether you have correctly entered all of your regular expenses, in the correct amount, in one of the four weekly periods. If you haven't, it will tell you the amount that you are "off by."

Let's stop for a second and see what you have accomplished once you've completed steps 1 and 2. You have told the PouchPlan how much income you have and when it comes in each month. You have also told the PouchPlan how much your regular expenses are and when they come due each month. The PouchPlan can now tell you how much money to leave in your checking account from each paycheck in order to cover the expenses that are due. You are never going to have to give any of these regular expenses another thought until something changes. Because the PouchPlan has you set up ALL of your regular expenses as automatic pay items and makes sure they are funded by each paycheck, you have probably put well over half of your monthly living expenses on autopilot! Talk about freedom!

Your bank account is starting to change from a place where you park your money until you spend it to the place where you only put the amount of money necessary to pay your automatic payments. In the envelope system, one could consider it the "Automatic Payment" category. You will stop looking at your bank account to determine how much money you have to spend and start looking at it knowing everything in the bank account is committed to a financial obligation and is already spent. It is very important that you clearly understand the main function of a checking account in the PouchPlan is *your automatic payment fund*. Now, that doesn't mean you will have no money to spend on day-to-day expenses. The PouchPlan has you start using real cash as you build a new understanding—and new habits—of your spending requirements.

Using actual cash may be a new experience for many of you, and I understand your reservation of going back to an "old school" type of payment. But before you say you can't do that "cash thing," let me share some of the amazing power using cash will provide you. When you use cash, you actually *feel* the spending. Why do you think casinos use chips? So it doesn't feel like real money to you! You need to *feel* your spending and using cash accomplishes that requirement. Additionally, when you spend cash from a section of the pouch, the transaction automatically updates your balance available in that category. No math, no accounting, no receipt posting or anything else is required for you to have an up-to-date, real-time balance in each area of your budget. All you have to do is spend the cash. The same is true if you need to transfer cash from one category to the other. All the accounting and math is handled by the actual moving of the cash. I am going to address the risks associated with cash in later chapters, but in the meantime, let me assure you that with over twenty-plus years of use, we have never lost a single dollar of money because of using cash in the PouchPlan.

Setting up automatic bill payments and drafts will save you a ton of headaches, time, and money. If necessary, the bank will print a check, put it in an envelope with a stamp on it, and get it in the mail in time to arrive by the promised date. And they do it for no charge! A lot of insurance companies and utilities will give you a discount if you set up an auto pay feature for your bill. The truth is automatic bill payments have less risk and are more dependable and convenient than a traditional check put in the mail. We have used auto payments and bank drafts for over fifteen years and for thousands of payments. Not once have we had a problem that cost us any money. Direct deposit of paychecks, auto drafts by companies and banks that offer them, and auto electronic bill pay for all other regular expenses are great financial tools you need to use as you move from "ouch" to "pouch."

STEP 3: IRREGULAR EXPENSES

OK, let's keep moving forward on the list to step 3. The last part of setting up your PouchPlan is determining your "irregular" expenses each month. *Irregular expenses* are expenses that are not the same in amount and/or due date from month to month. Examples are your food, clothes, household items, gasoline, gifts, car repair, and entertainment. All *irregular* expenses are going to be paid from the pouch with cash. There is another commonality of *irregular* expenses and that is you are typically present when the transaction takes place. You are at the grocery store when you buy food; you are at the gas station when you buy gas; you are at the department store when you buy clothes. The benefit of having the cash with you is that the transaction is completed without any delay or hassle and you are on your way.

Because you have completed steps 1 and 2, you have a known amount to apply to your *irregular* expenses. The PouchPlan displays your budget balance at all times in the "Summary Box" on the top of the spreadsheet. Start with your food and household amounts and work your way down to the least important items/activities you have. How do you decide what is the right amount to plan on spending? Odds are you have not been tracking these expenses and you are going to have to "guesstimate." It's OK to do so. We had to do the same thing when we started the system. Go with your gut and then adjust as you get better feedback from the pouch. The other step you should take is to have a large (20 percent or more of your total *irregular* expenses) "Miscellaneous" category for the first several months. Your job is to fill in the section of the PouchPlan spreadsheet for *irregular* expenses with the description and amount until the "Summary Box" shows a zero balance.

Be kind to yourself as you set up *irregular* expense categories and amounts for the first time. These types of expenditures are the hardest to keep track of and therefore are also the hardest to get exactly right on your first try. Remember to include a "Miscellaneous" category! A good starting point is to enter into the spreadsheet what you THINK you spend on each category per month. Then adjust to what you WANT to spend on each; then to what you NEED to spend on each; and finally, what you HAVE to spend on each. While you make these changes, the PouchPlan spreadsheet displays a running total of how much you have left to spend or how much you have to cut out of your budget. You are working your way to a zero balance, and the spreadsheet gives you updated feedback constantly.

The PouchPlan's "Quick Start Instructions" will walk you through the process as you complete your spreadsheet. It is a fill-in-the-blank activity with guiding instructions for each step. You work your way from available income to a zero balance as you assign dollar amounts to each category. You keep assigning your dollars until they are all used up. A running total is always displayed for both the amount(s) needed and the amount available.

The majority of PouchPlan users find that once they have set up all their *regular expenses* to draft out of their bank account, the amount of actual cash required to meet their *irregular expenses* is much less than they expected. There are several nice benefits to this discovery. The amount of total cash in your pouch is reduced and therefore so is the exposure to loss by accident or theft. The number of categories requiring cash funding is reduced resulting in less space needed to contain the cash. This is one reason we found the coupon-sized folder very efficient and user-friendly. The pouch fits easily inside a midsized purse and people are used to customers pulling out coupon files at checkout, so no one is alerted to the cash in your possession.

As you prepare your first monthly budget, your *irregular expenses* will be the last ones you set up. These expenses will be the first ones you adjust as you get your budget in balance. The reason you adjust your *irregular* expenses first is that you have more control over these than your *regular* expenses. Many *regular* expenses are commitments that you must meet. It is easier to change your entertainment or clothing expenses than it is your house or car payment. You may well decide that a major change in living is the right choice, but putting that into effect may require weeks or months to accomplish. (We have an entire chapter on tips to help you balance your budget.)

Irregular expenses will be fluid and flexible. They will change more often and in greater amounts than your *regular* expenses. As our kids got older, their school expenses climbed to the stratosphere. We went from field trips to the library or aquarium for $5 to summer trips to Washington DC! Dress-up days as fictional or historical characters cost just a few dollars while drill team and cheerleader uniforms cost hundreds. I remember that "School" was our second-largest category during the years we had three kids in high school. They were great days full of awesome memories, and the PouchPlan helped us handle their financial challenges.

STEP 4: BALANCING YOUR BUDGET

Your budget must balance. You have to get your summary of expenses and income to zero. We actually have the system's checks set to +/-$2.00 due to rounding. It is also OK if you get your total summary down to less than +/- $5.00. More about this tip later, but try to shoot for a zero balance and you will be in great shape. Think, "Every Dollar has a Duty." Start with adjusting the *irregular expenses* and then consider the *regular expenses*. If you have extra income, consider increasing your savings or the amount you put into your "Miscellaneous" category. You can do this. Keep moving the summary total toward zero with adjustments that make financial sense to you.

Sometimes, it is best to let the budget "rest" for a couple of days and then return and look at your situation with fresh eyes. If it is a family budget, it is OK for each spouse to prepare an estimate of irregular needs and priorities. Bring those two lists together and see where they are the same and where the priorities vary. Spouses are usually surprised by the amount of common rankings. Couples who attempt to understand the reasons behind the differences work them out quickly and gain new insight into their spouses.

Let's fast forward to when you reach ZERO. Take a deep breath and consider what you have accomplished. You have pushed the 800-pound gorilla out of the room, and you are now in charge! You have invested a couple of hours in yourself, and those hours are going to have an unbelievable payback.

In the next two chapters, I will give you the most powerful tools to help insure your success using the PouchPlan. Here is a little preview: People who have a WRITTEN plan and refer to that plan on a REGULAR basis have NINE TIMES more wealth than those who have no plan at all. You are now in the top 4 percent of all Americans and in the top ½ of a percent of all people on this planet. You have a plan!

PART 2

What Are the Necessary Ingredients for a Financial Foundation?

Part 2 is designed to give you the power to make the PouchPlan your financial foundation. In this part, I will share with you many of the principles that I and others have successfully used to make changes and progress in different and challenging circumstances. You will find motivational truths that you can relate to and just maybe have a couple of "Oh, my!" moments as I describe situations you probably believed were unique to you. We are all a lot more alike than we realize.

I quote and tell the stories of some really smart people in part 2. These people have dedicated their lives to looking past the default answers to finding the true reasons of our behaviors. Take their wisdom and apply it liberally to yourself and you can produce the outcomes you desire.

CHAPTER 3

You Gotta Have a Plan

I call this the PouchPlan on purpose. "If you don't have a plan for your money, you can be sure others do. And their plan will beat your 'no plan' every time." That quote came from my friend, Steve Stroope. Having a plan is critical to your success. Here is the simple truth: A weak plan will beat no plan, a good plan will produce great results, and an excellent plan can take you almost anywhere you want to go. Let's look at some fascinating statistics about what happens when you plan.

THE POWER OF A PLAN

According to a study at Virginia Tech, 80 percent of people do not have a financial plan or goal. Of the 20 percent who declare they have plans, 15 percent have never written down their plans or goals while only 4 percent have made the effort to write their goals down. Slightly less than 1 percent of these people have written goals that they review on a regular basis (once a month). What do you think is the difference in wealth between the 80 percent who have no plans and the 1 percent who have written and regularly reviewed goals? Do you think having a plan makes you 50 percent more productive? How about *twice* as productive as someone without a plan, a 100 percent increase? Do you believe having a plan could possibly produce an increase in your wealth by 300 percent?

May I have the envelope and a drum roll please? The Virginia Tech study showed a 900 percent wealth difference between the planners and the nonplanners! The 1 percent who had plans and regularly reviewed them made nine times as much money as those with no plans. The PouchPlan contains both these activities. You write your number plan on the spreadsheet and you review it every time you have a payday or an expense. Let's apply this statistic to an American's 2016 average income of $30,206 and do some math. This just might blow your mind!

By taking $30,206 and increasing it by nine fold, you come up with $271,854 per year in earnings. Now that is not what the study proves. But there are a couple of statistical tools—regressive analysis and the 80/20 Power Curve—that can project a reasonable estimate of income for the planners. That analysis shows a 90 percent chance of your income being double that of your peers.

Let's look at the numbers from another viewpoint. What is the real value of each hour of time it takes to make and then keep up a plan? Most PouchPlan users have been able to set up their first budget plan in a couple of evenings without their TV blaring in the background. I will use four hours as the average time required. The upkeep/review needs are only about twenty minutes per month or another four hours per year. This takes us a total of eight hours for the first year. How much are each of these eight hours you invest in the PouchPlan worth? Another drum roll, please. Based on the probability of doubling your income, how does $4,236 per hour sound?

Does this mean that your income is going to go up by 100 percent in the first year? I wish I could tell you yes, but the Virginia Tech study did not include a time frame detailing how long it takes for the difference in income to develop. I can just tell you that it does develop. Another fair question from the study is, did the financial plan cause the increase? The study proves correlation, not necessarily causation. I'm not trying to be all slimy here and give you a bunch of BS disclaimers. But, we are dealing with human behavior and its many, many aspects that affect outcomes. What my experience has taught me is the same type of "magical multiplying" effect that money possesses also comes from having a plan. And when you add them together, money plus a plan, you get multiplication times multiplication of your results, not just addition.

Here are a couple of examples from real life that should help you understand this concept. Remember how I mentioned that my wife and I have never had a heated discussion over money since we adopted the PouchPlan? In his book, *The Millionaire Mind*, Thomas A. Stanley writes that 92 percent of millionaire households in America consist of married couples. These millionaire couples also have a divorce rate of about 20 percent. Contrast these numbers to the American public in general. Less than 50 percent of the adult population is married, and the divorce rate is 58 percent for first-time marriages. We've already established the earning power of those who plan, so who do you think end up being millionaires, those who earn $30,206 per year or those who earn $271,854? Obviously, the ones with a plan have a much better chance of becoming millionaires. Just as obvious is the fact that those who marry and stay married make up the vast majority of millionaires. It is not a difficult step to conclude that having and following a financial plan helps marriages, as well as finances, succeed.

I really believe what is happening is much bigger than just some statistics. As your plan improves one thing, other things seem to improve as well. Financial control decreases stress in your life. Decreased stress makes communication easier. Better communication leads to understanding, and understanding shows respect. Respect leads to admiration, and admiration of another's qualities is a sign of love. I absolutely know there is a correlation between your happiness at home and your happiness everywhere else. I am convinced the PouchPlan positively impacts my relationship with my wife and therefore makes my life much better in many ways.

The next example of gaining more than expected involves a single mom who had a debt consolidation loan, a payday loan, and a seller-financed car loan. Maria had a clerical job that paid her on the first and fifteenth of each month. She had been cashing her check and driving twenty minutes to make her car payment and then another twenty minutes to make her payday loan and pay the babysitters. On the first payday of each month, she added another hour paying rent, her debt consolidation loan, cell phone, and other utilities. All totaled, she said she spent at least three hours each month just making her payments.

When we talked to her about changing her bank account to the "bill payment" account, she struggled to believe that her bank would really pay all these bills of hers. We assured her they would and that the bills would be paid on time. We had her log on to her bank account and helped walk her through the setup process for a couple of her bills. Then she said something we did not expect.

"What do I do next month when these come due?"

My wife caught on before I did and smiled and said, "Maria, you do the same thing we do, nothing. You will leave the money in the bank that the PouchPlan tells you to, and the bank will send the payments out each and every time until you tell them to stop."

Now the light goes on in Maria's head as she gets an excited look on her face. "Are you telling me that I don't have to fill out these bank forms and this budget each month?"

Her smile grew from ear to ear, and she began hopping up and down and squealing. We joined in on her celebration because we now understood. If you've been a single parent you know how hard it is to find even ten minutes of time in an all-consuming cycle of working, parenting, housekeeping, cooking, laundry, home repairs, car repairs, and every other responsibility two parents usually share. Maria had actually not done a single thing on her budget when she realized that just doing the plan was going to give her back at least three hours per month. She also understood she would only be spending fifteen to twenty minutes per month on her budget, not the two hours she was willing to give up to get her financial life in order. Now that time was hers as well. Maria decided she would split this newfound time between her kids and growing her part-time business. Oh, yes; Maria's part-time business pays her almost fifteen times the hourly rate of her clerical job.

Please grasp what I am telling you: *You can expect dramatic and disproportionally positive results from putting a doable and usable plan in place.* I am not saying you will become a millionaire, find the perfect spouse, or solve all of life's challenges in one fell swoop. But, your chances for achieving these and other important life opportunities increase as certain activities and behaviors are put in place. You have the opportunity to either make your life easier or to make it more difficult. Having a usable and doable financial plan will make almost all areas of your life easier.

Next, let's take a look at the attributes of, or what goes into, a great plan. I occasionally hear people mumbling that they do not want to "lose spontaneity" and "be trapped" by a plan. Planning does not inhibit you; it is a tool that enables you to live in abundance. If you wanted to spend an afternoon of loving and laughing with your son or daughter who lives five miles away, wouldn't you use the tool of the automobile to reduce a two-hour walk to a ten-minute drive? Of course you would. A plan is just another type of tool. A good one will add abundance to the laughter and love in your life.

THE ABCS OF PLANNING

I like and recommend the ABC model to help set up a plan. It is simple, covers the big areas you need to make sure are considered, and keeps you focused on progress. *A* = Accuracy; *B* = Begin; *C* = Change. This model can be used for all types of planning. I used it to become an author, and I used it to help me raise my children into functioning adults. You get a big head start when using this model on your financial plan as numbers or money naturally flow into accurate points. You will spend more time and effort when you try to accurately determine the goals of your relationships and family, career, and long-term finances. The PouchPlan is all about foundations, and this plan model is a great basic tool to help you begin to improve your foundation immediately.

A = Accuracy

Numbers force us to be accurate. You can't add or subtract the amount of "about $20," but you can add or subtract exactly $20. Your budget has to be "in balance." *In balance* means that the total income matches the total expenses. I like the expressions, "Every Dollar has a Duty" and "No Dollar Left Behind." A budget that does not have a plan for every dollar of income will end up leaking to death. You have achieved accuracy when you plan where every dollar of income is to be used.

Another feature of having an accurate focus is to hit the target you are shooting at. On your first budget, *your target should be to understand where your money is going and to decide if you like the results of your current situation.* That's all you need to accomplish with your first budget. After a short period of time, typically three to four pay cycles, you will have enough actual spending activity to move from "guesstimate" to "firm" estimate on your living expenses and spending habits. Once you have confidence in your spending information, you adjust your budget's target. You may want to establish an emergency fund, pay off debt, or start saving for college, a house, a car, a wedding, or retirement. What you choose to aim for will be personal and will require some soul-searching and prioritizing on your part. Adjusting your target will become second nature as you become experienced with the PouchPlan.

We have changed our target dozens of times over the last twenty-five years, and you should expect to as well. Life is going to throw you some surprises. Your needs and desires will also change and mature. When you use the PouchPlan, you have a great tool to help you make those decisions because you can easily see the effect of your financial choices on all areas of your life. You are able to make the changes with a clear perspective of how the other areas of your finances will be impacted. You decide ahead of time what is most important for your money to achieve for you.

You should always keep in mind that the more precisely you define your target, the better you will be able to move toward its achievement. This is the "aim small, miss small" effect and is very true. If you aim for something very specific and miss it a little bit, you may still get most, if not all, of the benefits of hitting your target. You will experience this effect as you set up your first budget to simply balance your current spending with your current income.

Be careful about setting up a target that is too far away. When you start the PouchPlan, or any plan, you should plan based on the shortest period possible. The PouchPlan gives you instructions by paycheck and covers a monthly period. Concentrate on the time frame between paychecks or even weekly.

I grew up and still live in a rather rural part of Texas. Firearms are something that I've been around my entire life. We use them for getting rid of pests such as barn rats and armadillos digging up our yard to more threatening critters like coyotes and snakes. Gun safety and respect for the power of a firearm are first, foremost, and mandatory when I teach my children and grandchildren responsible firearm use. I did not hand them a rifle and set out a target three hundred yards away. They started out with a BB gun at ten yards. The shots were all over the place, but every time they hit the paper, they were excited, and they learned by seeing where the BB hit. Pretty soon, most of their shots were hitting the paper, and eventually, through practice and experience, they gained the skills to hit the bull's eye. Keep the target close until your skill and experience grow. You can count on getting feedback from your misses until you hit the target.

B = Begin

That about covers the ***A***, so let's move to ***B***. You must begin! I recently heard a quote but I cannot seem to find out who originated it: "The world does not pay you for what you know; it pays you for what you do." You can never unleash the power of any plan until you take action on it. Will your plan work? You will not know for sure until you try it. Is your plan the best one ever? Probably not. But if you have a close-enough target, you can see where you missed. Remember the earlier idea that a person with a plan will beat a person with no plan? If you do not put your plan into action, it is the same thing as not having a plan.

A short aside here to handle another common reason I've heard for not following a plan: "I don't know how to get from where I am to where I want to go." That is OK; just follow someone who does. That's right; copy the most successful person you know who has achieved the same thing you are after. When I was a headhunter, the firm I worked for had the motto, "Fail Our Way First." Since they were in the top ten among thousands of recruiting franchises nationally, I bought in. Following their plan, I was rookie of the year in the southwest region and in the top twenty nationally my first year. I'd never recruited anybody for anything in my life before that job.

You need to realize that when you choose to follow someone else's plan, you then become the owner of that plan. You decide if parts of the plan are consistent with your values or not. Your specific situation may call for some, if not many, adjustments to make the plan accomplish the goals *you* want. When you are the one who is receiving the feedback from the actions you take, you are in the best position to make any adjustments based on your unique situation. By all means, pick the plan that you think will best serve you based on your needs and the plan's previous success achieving those goals but also please take ownership and responsibility for all of your actions and the output generated by your actions.

Let's get back to taking action. I will use the PouchPlan as an example of how you would start this process. Get an expandable coupon folder. Find your last two bank statements and/or your checkbook. Download the free spreadsheet and latest "Quick Start Guide" from www.PouchPlan.com. If you don't have a computer, get a thumb drive and go to your local library and use their computers. If nothing else, print the sample and master pages and use a #2 pencil to fill in your budget! To quote the hockey legend Wayne Gretzky, "You miss 100 percent of the shots you don't take."

Beginning your plan or budget is a lot like driving at night. When you start out, you cannot see all the way to your destination. As a matter of fact, your headlights only show you what is a couple of hundred feet down the road. This limitation doesn't stop you from heading to the grocery store or the movies. As you drive down the road, a new two hundred feet appear within your view, and you take prudent actions to continue on toward your goal. You repeat this process until you arrive at your destination. If you just begin by taking the action right in front of you—the one you believe will produce the best outcome for you—you will constantly be moving toward your chosen destination. Then choose the next action that keeps you on track and continue this process until you arrive successfully at your destination. This is a great place to move on to the next part of the model, ***C,*** Change.

C = Change

You change your plan based on feedback. Consider this example. I have found the contrast between these two famous sayings rather humorous: "If at first you don't succeed, try, try again" and "The definition of insanity is doing the same thing over and over and expecting different results." Occasionally, when I'm bored or around someone who is pretty full of himself, I like to combine the two sentences into one and see people's reactions. (Sorry, that's a poor example of feedback. Funny as heck, but a poor example.)

Here is a much better example. Perry Marshall wrote an excellent book called *80/20 Sales and Marketing*. In his book, he described how he became the go-to expert on Google Adwords. In a nutshell, he took a proven method of split-testing two ads to see which produced the better results and then keeping the better of the two. But he did not stop there. He tested the better add against a new one. Sometimes, the newer ad might only be a change to the sentence structure or a single word. He continued this process of testing the winner against a new challenger dozens and dozens of times and picking the new winner based on feedback. Eventually, he would find the combination that produced two, four, or even ten times the response his competitors' ads were achieving. At this point, his competitors were no longer competitive with him. When you increase your performance tenfold by simply following the feedback, you will be able to dominate the unmanageable in your life. Perry Marshall is probably one of the top ten people on the planet for writing effective ads. He still looks at his results, listens to feedback, then makes adjustments every time. You should, too.

When one of our PouchPlan users, Jamie, wanted to increase her savings, we suggested she look at making some small but repeatable changes. Jamie was spending about $4.50 per sugar-free caramel latte at her Starbucks, stopping by an average of three or four days per week. I'm not a coffee connoisseur. I like mine black and McDonald's or 7-Eleven is fine for me. I certainly do not begrudge anyone enjoying something that adds to her enjoyment of life, especially if she can afford it, and Jamie absolutely could do so. But the numbers were right there in front of me, and I just could not keep my mouth shut.

"Why don't you cut out the Starbucks?"

I'm not going to tell you what she suggested I cut out. But I think I would rather dine with Hannibal Lecter than spend time with this young lady without her Starbucks.

I tried to choose my next words very carefully as they might be my last.

"OK, you love your Starbucks. But do you love the product or the Starbucks experience?"

After about five seconds, her ice-cold death stare transferred from between my eyes into space. Her trust level was low, but she was willing to take another couple of steps. Very slowly, she said it was probably the coffee. Although the customer service was excellent, she still had to wait between ten and fifteen minutes in the drive-through on most visits. She quickly followed up that the wait was worth it, and that I should understand with only about three visits per week, she felt like she had already cut back.

Neither of us could come up with a solution she liked. We agreed to both think about options and then get together again in about a week. She got in touch with me a couple of days later and said she was looking at some single-serving coffee machines. I had used one at a company I worked for and thought it was an interesting idea. As I researched types, I found a brand that used a two-disc process and was capable of foaming milk for lattes and hot chocolates. I sent her the link and she checked it out.

As luck would have it, Amazon had the machine on sale for $119, and the lattes would cost about $1.40 per serving. A quick look at the numbers told us she would save $500 the first year after paying for the coffeemaker. After the first year, the savings would be $620 annually. The question she had to answer was if the quality of the latte would satisfy her Starbucks expectations. It was really interesting to watch her work through that question. In the end, she decided that she would try the machine for two months (which covered the cost due to the savings), and if she didn't think it was a suitable substitute for her Starbucks drink, she would throw away the machine, return to Starbucks for her lattes, and follow through with her threat to me!

The story has a very happy ending. She liked the coffeemaker lattes very much. She loved saving the money. She says she underestimated the reduction in stress and the positive benefits of gaining thirty to forty minutes of morning time each week and that alone might be worth the change. Jamie still stops by a Starbucks every now and then, especially if she is out of town.

I will agree that this scenario took some effort to resolve, but here are the probable results of making this one small change. Jamie was twenty-eight years old when she made this change. If she continues to save that $620 each year until she retires at sixty-five, that consistent, small change will result in an increase of $145,000 in her retirement account. Jamie will tell you that Starbucks's coffee is a little better than what she makes, but no way is it $145,000 better!

The story actually gets better. Over the next four or five years, there was a product shortage for the discs in the coffeemaker and they were unavailable. Jamie's husband was already grinding and making his own coffee every morning, so she found a device that heated and whipped milk into a latte. She also located syrups in her favorite flavors. As of now, she says her cost is below $0.75 per drink and she has them EVERY morning. I promise you that we laugh out loud when we think back to that first conversation.

In this chapter, I have been trying to demonstrate to you the power of a plan. It is one of those tools that provides you an amazing multiplying effect. You jump past addition and even multiplication into the realm of exponential impact. You know that 4 + 4 = 8. You know that 4 x 4 = 16, twice the result. But did you ever consider that 4^3 is equal to 48, a 600 percent increase over addition? When you combine the magical multiplier of money with a plan, you will begin to see how the most amazing results can be yours.

CHAPTER 4

Willpower Fails but Habits Rule: Take Charge of Your Money in 60 Days!

Willpower is way overrated. Most people do not fall off the personal financial wagon during the ride; they fall off while trying to get on. If you can get up and on, the chances of your staying on are actually pretty good. This chapter is about the amazing power of habits and how to harness that power for turning your budget and financial plan into reality. You are going to depend very little on your willpower because, quite honestly, it just doesn't work. I'm going to share with you how you can make the PouchPlan your normal way of functioning when it comes to directing your financial life. I'm going to introduce you to several techniques that will have you using the PouchPlan just like you use air for breathing—automatically and without thought. In other words, the PouchPlan will become your habit.

Here are some characteristics of *habits*: They are strong and hard to break. They use very little mental energy and allow us to focus on other opportunities. They provide consistent and repetitive behaviors and actions. They can be created, changed, or replaced. Habits are actually shortcuts taken by our brains. Brains love them and do everything they can to make more of them. Habits are a lot like money; they are *amoral*; that is, they are neither immoral nor moral. The truth is we determine whether our habits produce good or bad results.

Here are some characteristics of *willpower*: It has limited endurance. It requires lots of mental energy to support. It requires concentration and limits our focus on other challenges. Willpower produces inconsistent results and behaviors. What is sad is that for almost any negative result dealing with effort, *more willpower* is constantly held up as the cure. Well, they are right about one thing: Willpower is a lot of effort; habits are a bunch of ease.

THE STRUCTURE OF A HABIT

A habit has three parts: First is the *stimulus* or *event*; you can also call this a *trigger* or *cue*. The trigger or cue can be something as simple as waking up in the morning when you smell the coffee to something as complex as your relationship with your parents. The stimulus can be physical, mental, or emotional. The second part is your *action* or *response* to the stimulus. Your response can also be physical, mental, or emotional, and it does not have to be the same type as the stimulus. Your brain is attempting to put this part, your response, on autopilot. The third part of the structure of a habit is the *reward* you receive. Once again, the reward can be physical, mental, emotional, or any combination of the three.

Once you have accepted the reward as sufficient, your brain begins to make the response into your default behavior, then into your automatic behavior, and finally into the unconscious behavior you know as a habit. Your brain is happy; it no longer has to put much effort into the response. You are happy receiving the reward while expending much less mental energy. As this cycle repeats itself, the habit becomes stronger and more resistant to change. Are you beginning to understand why a habit is much more powerful than willpower? I can guarantee you that someone who seems to have a lot of willpower really has a habitual behavior that is running unnoticed in the background. *Our challenge is to harness this power of habits, add to it the power of a plan, and then have it all multiplied by the power of money.*

Here are the best techniques I've seen for establishing or changing habits. I will also walk you through how the PouchPlan uses each technique to transform your budgeting process into a habit. The first technique is to remove the trigger or cue. The second technique is to put obstacles between you and the default response. The third technique is to take the smallest action that moves you toward your desired behavior.

You probably noticed that I left out the one skill that everyone knows about: repetition. I will admit that repetition is, by definition, the major part of a habit. When you are trying to establish or overhaul a habit, repetition, assisted by willpower and motivation, still usually results in frustration and failure. You already know from statistics regarding New Year's resolutions they have a pitiful success rate of between 5 and 8 percent. I would like to see that percentage increased by a factor of ten for PouchPlan users. I'm laughing a bit as I write this because odds are you already have a habit of using repetition to try to form new habits! That's OK. We are going to use the power of repetition, but it is going to be the icing on the cake, not the main ingredient.

TRIGGERS AND CUES

The power of removing a cue is almost 100 percent effective. The classic example is how you pay your taxes. Do you think the government would get much cooperation if they sent someone around on payday to get taxes from each person? Obviously not. The reason they get so much money with so little complaining is they remove YOU from the transaction. The tax is taken out before you even have a chance to put your hands (and mind) on the money. I do not mean to sound cynical, but this tactic is so effective that when you get back what you have overpaid, you are very happy with your "refund."

Alcoholic Anonymous uses the same technique with a different twist. You change friends and social situations. Most drinkers get together with other drinking friends at a bar or other places where alcohol is readily available. In AA, you meet a new friend (a *sponsor*) and a group of other friends (the other people at the AA meetings) to socialize with and to be accepted by without the presence of alcohol. These people and places provide the opportunity to meet the tremendous human need of social interaction and acceptance with most of the triggers of the bad habit removed. (I checked up on the latest studies for this example, and per the National Institute of Health as of 2015, there is no addiction treatment that outperforms AA or NA [Narcotics Anonymous]. Oh, yeah; participation in both is free.)

The PouchPlan uses a combination of both of the above examples as we remove the triggers causing unwanted and uncontrolled spending. First, we remove the opportunity and need to decide what to do with your money now that you have it. You follow the predetermined instructions for each paycheck. There is no decision required on your part as you sit with your paycheck in your hand. You simply follow the instructions that were predetermined by your wants and needs based on what *you* decided were the most important. You made these decisions with the big picture of your life clearly in view. These decisions were made with the consequences right in front of you. You can trust yourself.

Second, you will only invite a special group of friends (categories) that have the same goals as you do to your spending party. You've given these friends proper boundaries (amounts) so your relationships stay healthy. You now get to celebrate the experience of spending time and going to places with your new friends knowing that the rewards you expect are coming your way. These rewards can be anything from paying for quality child care to a great night's rest to funding an around-the-world cruise. The really cool thing about this behavior is the more time you spend with your friends, the better off you are.

ERECTING BARRIERS AND OBSTACLES

The next technique is to use *barriers* or *obstacles.* Retail clothing stores are experts at this technique. They have you walk by all the professionally displayed latest fashions with perfect lighting and mirrors so you can see how good you look in these high-margin items as you head to the back of the store for the sales rack. There is nothing sinister about this tactic, just recognition of human behavior. By the way, it is very effective. Grocery stores do the same thing. Dairy, drinks, and meats will be at the back of the store, and candy, chips, and pharmacy items are usually toward the front. If nothing else, you have to walk past these higher-margin products twice, and stores are hopeful you're running on only willpower that day.

I love these next couple of examples of obstacles. The size of the obstacle can be miniscule and still have a very powerful effect. If you squash a roll of toilet paper so it doesn't "roll" easily, there will be a measurable difference in the amount of toilet paper people use. Google, who is famous for their snack-friendly office environment, decided the M&Ms they were providing were not the best nutritional choice available. They did not want to been seen as "taking away" something, so they decided to change the M&Ms from clear-glass containers to opaque ones. Just making it harder to see what was in the container resulted in less consumption of M&Ms and thus a decrease of three million calories over the next seven weeks for the two thousand employees in their New York office. The truth is what we often label as "lazy" our bodies and minds see as efficient and want to use. We just need to go with the flow rather than fighting it as we build new habits or change existing ones.

The PouchPlan uses the obstacle of *immediate consequences*, or *present pain*, to help keep you on track. I'm not talking about physical pain but the emotional experience of loss. And remember that sometimes just a tiny amount of an obstacle is enough to reduce the influence of a habits trigger. When you use the PouchPlan and want to change your spending, you have to physically remove the amount of cash from one category in order to fund the new spending choice. This requires you to see the dollars going out (pain associated with loss) of the planned category as you take this action. This is a no-brainer if you have to move cash from entertainment or travel in order to pay for a necessary plumbing repair. The hurt will kick in if you are considering moving gasoline money that you know you need for getting to your job into the "Hair Care" category because the coloring was not quite right on your new 'do.

I'm on really thin ice here talking about the "Hair" category of the pouch. I'm willing to do so because it shows how the mental and emotional parts of the PouchPlan unfold as you use it. I get my hair cut about every other month. It costs me $15, and I usually tip $5 for a total of $20. My wife's hair care is at a totally different level. I have heard her call it a "cut," "cut and color," "style," "cut and style," and a couple of more phrases that I can't pronounce. Our "Hair" category gets $60 each month. All I know is that $10 of that is for me because I get my hair cut every other month. The other $50 per month is fair game for my wife to spend however she chooses. And let me tell you...she takes her choices (and her hair) very seriously. She knows exactly how much each of the hair-care options costs, how often she needs to have each service preformed, and how difficult it is to get a rescheduled appointment if she has to change it. She can be thinking two or three months ahead about how she plans on spending from this category.

If I suggest we move money from the hair-care section, I might as well be asking to use Grandpa's ashes to fertilize the front lawn. My wife is now making an emotional connection with the loss of her future hair care in real time as the cash is taken out of the pouch. The pain is real and is now associated with the current choice being made. A real obstacle has been created. By having this emotional connection happen in real time, you will be encouraged to make the decision that is the least painful overall, not just moving the pain of the choice to the future where you can hope it goes away. By physically moving the money, you have to make sure the "plus" of where you are moving it to results in a more positive for you than the negative of losing the activity you are taking it from. By moving the consequences of the future into your current emotions, you have created an obstacle to unwanted behavior or habits.

As you use the PouchPlan, you will develop an almost sixth sense about the tradeoffs that must be made. Life is going to throw you some curves. As you reach into, say, the "Clothes" section to fund a new and wanted school activity, you will be mentally preparing yourself to ignore the latest fashion display and head straight to the sales rack. That is a trade-off you were willing to make because you wanted your child to experience something special. You know it is worth it, so go ahead and smile in that mirror.

One more type of obstacle I want you to consider establishing is *peer pressure*. If you are a couple or family using the PouchPlan, it will be there automatically and should be taken advantage of. You may want to use the word "accountability," as it has less of a negative sense. I know sharing your financial information with another person can be a scary or humbling experience. But if there is someone you know and trust, especially if you both are trying to make the same improvements in your lives, the potential for your success will increase dramatically by adding an accountability component. Let me share with you just how powerful this obstacle to habitual triggers can be.

Humans are conditioned to tell the truth. When we lie, a bunch of our physical norms change. Our blood pressure goes up, our breathing changes, we sweat, we blink, we look away; even the temperature of our fingertips changes. Some people do get better at hiding these physical reactions, but they are still there and can be measured. All of this and much more is documented and well known. Our default behavior is to tell the truth.

In 1956, a gentleman by the name of Solomon Asch came up with an ingenious way of testing the power of peer pressure. He asked a question with a multiple-choice answer option in front of a group. The question was very simple, and it was very obvious the correct answer was *B*. Students were asked the question one at a time and were instructed to give their answers out loud in front of the group after they were asked the question. But there was a catch. The first six students were in on the test and had been instructed by Mr. Asch to answer *A*, the obviously wrong answer, in a strong and clear voice. Would student number seven knowingly lie to fit into the group? And the answer is....You bet! An astonishing 75 percent of the time. The same results have been produced as this experiment has been repeated over one hundred times in fifteen-plus countries over the last fifty years. The power of peer pressure is overwhelming. (This might make you want to consider who you are hanging around with. Just saying ☺.)

How are you going to bring in this power of peer pressure to help you be successful with the PouchPlan? It is built-in if you put your plan together with your spouse or significant other. You've each made the commitment that this is the plan you are going to follow. The accountability is in plain sight as spending takes place. It is really hard to hide and requires deliberate deception to pull off. If that is what is going on in your relationship, you have bigger problems to handle than just money. Intentionally deceiving someone you care about is a difficult emotional action. It is just the kind of obstacle we are looking to take advantage of.

If you are doing the PouchPlan by yourself, you can still create accountability by sharing your goals and commitments with someone you trust, perhaps a parent or a lifelong friend. You might want to consider a professional, like an accountant, counselor, or minister. I think you will find most people are receptive to the idea of assisting someone to better him- or herself. I once asked a guy to help me whom I had known for about two months. I had to give him my debit card for the week because I could not account for where all my cash had been spent the previous week. He is now a friend of twenty-five years whom I greatly admire, and I am extremely thankful for his coming alongside of me in my time of need.

SMALL CHANGES, BIG RESULTS

Tactic number 3 is to make very small changes. Our brains don't seem to get excited about small changes. But small changes can be stacked one on top of another for gigantic results. A life insurance company back in the '90s recruited its employees to participate in a "get fit" study. All the employees on one floor (approximately one hundred employees) were offered free gym memberships and workout clothing. The employees on another floor were asked to walk just one flight of stairs per day. They could increase the number of flights of stairs if they wanted to, but it was not required or even requested.

At the end of one year, less than 20 percent of the people who were given the gym membership had visited the gym in the previous month. The stair walkers were a different story. Almost 50 percent of this group was doing some type of daily physical activity for twenty minutes or more. The first group had lost no weight, and the second group had lost an average of four pounds per person. There was a core group of twenty-five-plus walkers who met each day for lunch and walked the stairs of all twenty-eight floors of their building. More than ten had run a 5K race, and two were training for a marathon! These are some pretty good results from the original commitment of about one minute.

There were a lot of positive behaviors going on in the

above results, and it is not fair to assume all the success was due to the small initial request. Both groups had the same opportunity to use the power of peer pressure and the power of commitment. Only the walkers had the major advantage, being instructed to start small. When you start small, you take away the fear of failure; you guarantee success. It doesn't have to be a huge success, just one you can repeat and then build upon.

As you start the PouchPlan, you are doing exactly what you were doing before, spending your money. We are just going to arrange how the spending takes place in a slightly different way. This is true because all you are trying to do with your first PouchPlan budget is to determine where your money is going. As you gain experience (success and feedback), you can decide if you like where your money is going. If you don't, you can direct it where you want it to go as your options and consequences become clearer. As the habit forms, you begin to take more steps and make more progress almost without effort.

Time to put the icing on this cake. We have taken away the triggers that have caused you to have poor spending habits. We have built obstacles to old behaviors with the addition of new friends with limits. We have established small, familiar-type steps to start the process. We are going to take the hardest part of building a habit and make it simple and automatic, which is repetition. *Repetition is required for a behavior to become a habit.* You start this repetition building every time you spend from a pouch section—automatically. You reinforce repetition every time you put money into, or move it out of, a section—automatically. Even a quick glance to see how much is available in a particular section adds to the repetitive behavior—automatically. And last of all is my personal favorite: You automatically build this habit when you do NOT look at your bank balance because you know the money in there has already been assigned a spending responsibility.

If you will follow these examples, you will find yourself with new and improved spending behaviors in around sixty days. And they will be your new habits—your default and automatic behaviors. You will have broken through to a whole new area in your financial life. You will now be in charge of your money.

CHAPTER 5

Passing along Lessons from Real Life

LESSONS FROM CAPITALISM AND CHRISTIANITY

I previously mentioned there are tremendous amounts of resources corporations (and governments) pour into planning activities each year. The reason they continue to do so is because it works. I am going to ask you to take a deep breath and slow down just a bit while I share with you the biggest lesson I learned from my years in corporate America. It is a sinkhole that captured way too many smart and talented people. Some paid for this mistake with their careers and others sacrificed a lot more.

If you have all the best tools, the best people, and the best plans, but have a *misplaced* or *adulterated target*, you are going to fail miserably. You will also hurt the majority of those around you. What is a "misplaced" or "adulterated target"? It is one that on the surface seems to be legitimate but when examined in detail produces outcomes that are against the original values and goals you set out to achieve. Even if you start out with a great goal, this change in focus can creep in over a period of time. *The longer any entity is in existence, the more likely it is that its primary purpose becomes its self-perseveration instead of its original reason for existing.*

The vast majority of people I worked with were quality individuals whom I could count on to do the right thing consistently. Sadly, it seemed there was always a minority who tried to use deceit or deception as cover for poor results. The excuse they would give was usually something like, "We need to live to fight another day." The lesson most people learned was it was OK to lie if the results were in your favor. What I soon discovered was if "they" were willing to lie to others, "they" were willing to lie to me.

I was buying cars at an auction one evening when a floor spotter came and stood by me. Floor spotters help the auctioneer recognize bidders. The staff all knew me as I had been buying and selling vehicles there for about a year. The spotter called out several bid acceptances, and then I realized he was using me as the bidder.

I leaned over and told him I was not bidding, and he just winked and immediately accepted a new, higher bid! It took me about five seconds to put it all together. The auction was rigged! Once they thought you were on their side, they let you in on the secret. The vehicle sold to another bidder, but he had paid about $500 more than its true market value. I had probably bought two hundred cars at that auction. I wondered how many times I had not been in on the secret. I never went back.

I hesitate to say it, but religion also gives us clear examples of this contamination effect on goals. Christianity moved from a religion began by a Savior who gave his life for the shortcomings of others to an organization that at one point in its history tortured and burned alive those who disagreed with it and were labeled "heretics." We see a similar behavior today as radical Islamists behead those who disagree with their religion and are labeled "infidels." (For those of you who don't know, *Islam* means "peace.")

I'm bringing this up because I want you to always remember the reason why you are putting a budget or financial plan together in the first place. You are investing this effort to make your life and the lives of those you care for better. With this book as your guide, you can use the PouchPlan as a tool to make great decisions. It is about people first and then the money. The money will likely be required to achieve your goals, but if you compromise the important people in your life to get it, you will regret that decision. (Read up on the last fifteen years of Howard Hughes's life if you need a visual.)

Please do not take this the wrong way. I will state unconditionally that Christianity and capitalism have done more to improve the lot of people than anything in history. Without them, the world would be a darker and poorer place. This is just a warning for those who need it. If you see that you are not making good progress with your plan and the people who are important to you are not on board, you may need to reassess how you are implementing your actions. Sometimes, in our zeal to hit our target, we can get pulled aside. This is very important if you are a couple or family. There is only one boat in these situations, and everyone needs to be rowing the same direction.

I have seen two actions that work effectively if you find yourself in this situation: One is a review of your target or goal. Is this goal still the primary thing you want to accomplish? Is your main thing still the main thing? A little bit of experience may have given you a better perspective and requires you to refine your target. It took me several years and plenty of mistakes before I realized my primary responsibility as a parent was to raise children who became competent, functioning adults. Sure, I wanted them to like me, be happy, feel secure, and get a great education. But those very positive things could not be my primary goals. If my children grew up to be dysfunctional adults who could not hold a job or enjoy close relationships, I had failed them. Fortunately, it is possible to love them all the way to their becoming really great grown-ups.

After you have reappraised your focus, set aside your judgments of everyone involved and check all the communication. Does everyone understand the how and why that went behind each decision? Plain ole ignorance can be assumed to be noncooperation or even sabotage if you let your imagination run unchecked. You would be surprised how many times people are not even in the same book, much less on the same page. Maybe you let your significant other walk you through the plan as he or she explains each category and amount. Listen to and try to understand his or her perspective. The Golden Rule is golden in situations like this. Take the time and effort to make sure the path you are on is leading to where you really want to end up and not some sinkhole to nowhere.

LESSONS FROM DIETING

I mentioned earlier that I am a numbers guy. Numbers make sense to me and talk to me and even affect me much like music in a weird sort of way. Yes, I can get emotional about a number. There is this one range of numbers that just seems to be a tipping point for me. It is 92-96 percent and its mirror sibling, 4-8 percent. When I see numbers in this range, I immediately get a gut feeling that something is either really, really, right or it's really, really, wrong. For example, if a political candidate gets 95 percent of the vote, I'd say something is really, really, wrong. Probably a totalitarian government posing as a democracy. On the other hand, if I see a 95 percent customer satisfaction rating on Amazon from verified users, I'm going to think it is a great product. I can count on it to perform its function at or above my expectations.

We've already seen the 96 percent number come up in this book. Remember that only 4 percent of people write down and review their financial goals on a regular basis, and these folks achieve wealth 900 percent higher than those who do not write down and review their goals. I found another number that caught my attention from a study done by the University of Scranton. It seems that 92 percent of New Year's resolutions are not achieved within one year. That is an astonishing failure rate. The top two resolutions are to lose weight and to exercise.

I understand that there is no direct correlation between those who diet and those who need to get their financial lives in order. I use dieting as an example because many of us are familiar with the activity. I've done so many diets that some members of my family consider it my favorite hobby! The numbers tell me that the failure rate of those who try to lose weight by dieting is very close to those who don't have a plan and fail to achieve financial success, and that piques my interest. In her amazing book, *Secrets from the Eating Lab*, Dr. Traci Mann writes, "If you find that most people behave the same way, then the explanation for their behavior has very little to do with the kind of people they are. It has to do with the circumstances in which they find themselves." Let's be honest. The circumstances in America today do not work with you as you try to eat better or to be financially responsible.

Reliable statistics on dieting success must be dug out of a pretty ugly pile. There are so many types of diets and so many claims from sources with a dog in the fight it can be hard to separate fact from fiction. But it seems to me the mental aspects of dieting are very similar to budgeting, and there is a lot more academic research on dieting than budgeting. Perhaps we can see what has and has not worked and pick up some helpful ideas.

What does work? Well, according to the same Dr.

Mann, there are three things you can do that put the odds of a successful diet change within reach. She makes a strong argument that you need to reduce or eliminate the availability of the food you do not want to eat by doing the following:

- Lower the temptation by erecting obstacles to obtaining the foods you do not want to eat.
- Make the food choices you want to eat available and noticeable.
- When possible, have the food choice you want to eat be the ONLY choice available.

Do you notice what is missing? Willpower. Notice what is there? A plan and a habit change.

I love Tim Ferriss and his *4-Hour* series of books. In the *4-Hour Body,* he tells the story of a man who did nothing but draw a line on a piece of graph paper representing the amount of weight he wanted to lose over a six-month period. The slope rate was about 0.10 percent per day. And I mean he did nothing. He weighed himself every morning when he woke up. Other than that, he went out of his way to make sure he did not change one single aspect of his life. He gave himself some leeway to reduce stress, but if he was above the line, he might cut out a dessert that day. If he was below the line, he would add some doughnuts and stuff himself back on course. He lost almost thirty pounds in six months and did it, as he said, "Without any effort."

What did we just see? Small, almost inconsequential actions were required. Anything else? Regular review of the results. Actually, most people would probably say that was a pretty lame plan. To me, it is another example that any plan, even a weak one, will beat no plan every time. I'm not going to even pretend these are the only forces at work in dieting or in making and sticking to a financial plan. But is often possible to look at groups of winners to see what common traits they share and then see if any of those traits can be used in your situation. If so, give them a try. That is what we did over the years as we lived with and improved the PouchPlan. That is what we now pass on to you.

PART 3

The Recipe—Putting Your PouchPlan Together

In this part, I will be showing you how to maximize your results from the PouchPlan. The PouchPlan is designed around income from a paycheck, expenses paid from a checking account, and by using cash out of your pouch. Many of you will have situations that vary from this design. Don't worry; we did, too. And so did a lot of other users of the PouchPlan. This part addresses those differences and gives you guidance and instructions on how to make the PouchPlan work for you. It has lots of chapters and sections to help you search for the specific area where you need help.

It is not necessary for you to read this entire part before you put your PouchPlan into action. If you get stuck putting your budget together, chapter 6 is the place to go if you have questions about your income.

Chapters 7 and 8 will address questions on expenses. It is a good idea to take the time to read the entire part 3 after you have used the PouchPlan for a couple of months. There are lots of time-saving and aggravation-reducing tips you will find in each chapter. We also have available a "Frequently Asked Questions" (FAQ) section on the website, www.pouchplan.com, which is a great source for those unique situations.

I have a special treat for those of you who do not like to read a bunch of instructions but want to make sure you don't miss the best tips or techniques. When describing a tip or technique that my wife or I thought really made a big difference for us, I will put the designation (**BTT**) in front of it. (**BTT**) represents **B**est **T**ips and **T**echniques. This will allow you to skim the chapters in seconds and still make sure you are exposed to these really great gems.

CHAPTER 6

Types of Income

Using the PouchPlan, you record your income by pay period or paycheck. The spreadsheet will then convert your pay to a monthly amount for budgeting against your total monthly expenses. I set it up this way because it is how real life works. Your money comes in to you on a different timetable than it goes out. The PouchPlan spreadsheet provides all the abracadabra as you fill in the how much and the when. Once you've done your part, all you do is follow the instructions provided for each paycheck.

This section is designed to answer some very specific questions users of the PouchPlan have asked. Not all, maybe very few, if any, will be necessary for the majority of people to know to put the PouchPlan into action. Do not get hung up on a concept or situation that you do not face. Just skip it. As a practical plan, you may just want to skim through by reading the

"Best Tips and Techniques" (**BTT**) alerts to see if you even need to consider a particular subject.

CONSISTENT OR REGULAR INCOME

If your pay is the same amount from period to period, the income section of the PouchPlan is a simple fill-in-the-blank process. You start with your gross check amount and then list all of your paycheck deductions to arrive at your net pay. (**BTT**) *If you don't want to itemize your payroll deductions, you can just enter your net pay or "take-home" as your income instead of your gross pay amount. If you choose to enter your net check, you do not have to enter any payroll deductions.* No matter which amount you use, make sure the drop-down box for "Pay Period" matches your actual pay period. (See Figure 6-1.)

6-1: Pay Period Drop-down Box

Click on the pay period to display arrow. Click on the arrow to see options and select pay period.

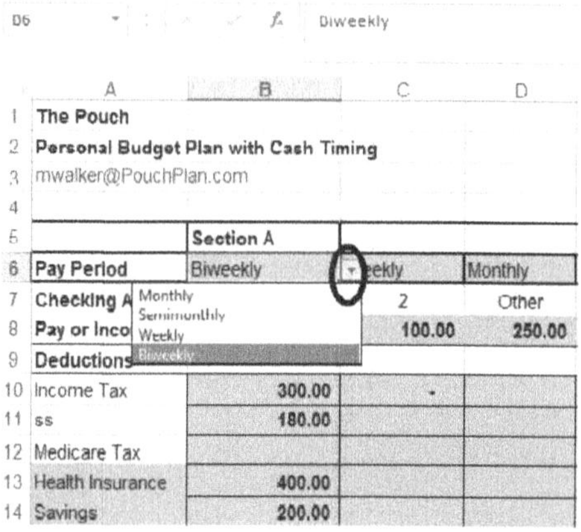

INCONSISTENT OR IRREGULAR INCOME

If your income varies by how much or how often, you will have to guesstimate an amount. You will need to follow a practice from the *Price Is Right* television show: Get as close as you can to the amount without going over! As a general rule, the longer the period you use for the estimate, the more accurate the forecast. For example, if I use only last week's paycheck and multiply it by fifty-two times to get an annual amount, I could be way off if last week is full of overtime. On the other hand, if I take the last three months' income and multiply by four, I probably pick up some checks with overtime and some without, resulting in a much closer projection of my annual income. It can be a disaster if you take only your best week (month, or quarter) for projections and do not include the reality of down cycles.

The other thing you are going to have to do is watch and make changes to your plan if your estimate is not proving to be accurate. It would be best to do this every month, but make sure you do this at least every ninety days. This is true if you miss way below or above your estimate. Making sure "Every Dollar has a Duty" is extremely important as you begin the PouchPlan.

Having a "Miscellaneous Expense" category is vital if your income varies. In these types of circumstances, it can absorb small variances without impacting other areas of your budget. (**BTT**) *Always print out a hard copy or save a copy to your computer of your current budget before you make any changes to it.* I can't tell you how many times I wish I had the "old" copy to compare to the new. If you don't print it or copy it, it is gone forever.

If your income varies greatly from month to month, which is common in many sales professions, you should take one additional step. Set up a separate savings account into which you deposit your income and take regular amounts out on a regular basis. This can be set up automatically at your bank. You set your budget up on the amount you regularly withdraw from your savings. (**BTT**) *This has been most successful when users of the PouchPlan set up semimonthly withdrawals. The main reason is it creates a good habit very quickly. Using a semimonthly period also reduces the amount of cash required to fund your pouch to a two-week period of time instead of four weeks.*

OTHER TYPES OF INCOME

Other income is money you receive that is not a part of your regular pay. I'm constantly surprised how many people have income that falls into this category. Examples of this would be retirement pensions, investment income, child support, dividends, welfare benefits, or an inconsistent part-time job or business. If it is a regular amount and received in regular intervals, all you do is convert it to a monthly amount and enter that total. If you are pretty sure of the annual amount but do not know exactly when it will come in, go ahead and use the annual amount divided by twelve for your monthly budget figure. There are drop-down boxes for the frequency of income at the top of the "Other Income" area just like there are above the "Paycheck" area. (See Figure 6-2.)

6-2: Other Pay Period Drop-down Box

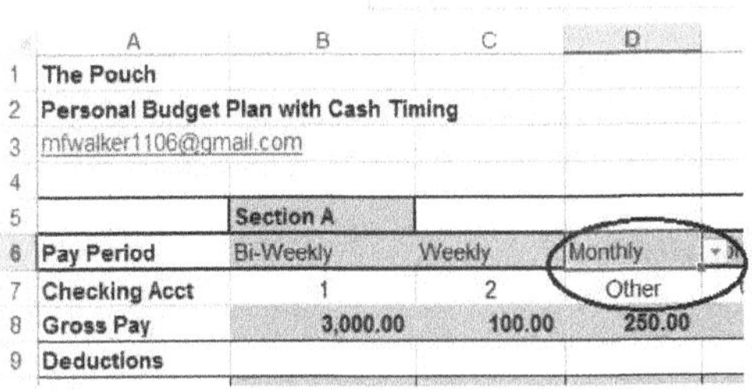

	A	B	C	D
1	The Pouch			
2	Personal Budget Plan with Cash Timing			
3	mfwalker1106@gmail.com			
4				
5		Section A		
6	Pay Period	Bi-Weekly	Weekly	Monthly
7	Checking Acct	1	2	Other
8	Gross Pay	3,000.00	100.00	250.00
9	Deductions			

Your other income is handled differently by the PouchPlan spreadsheet when it determines the funding of your pouch. The spreadsheet takes your paycheck information and your regular expenses and automatically enters them into section C, the "Pouch-Funding" section, from sections A and B. It does not do so with your other income amounts. You will need to manually enter your other income into section C on your own. Enter the amount of the other income into the column that matches the date the funds are available to you. This entry is made on line 64 of the spreadsheet. (See Figure 6-3.) Other income must be entered for the cash instructions per paycheck to be correct. An exception to these instructions is listed below if you receive the other income on a debit or credit card.

DEBIT CARD AND EBT INCOME

Several states offer child support and other benefits directly deposited onto a debit card rather than into a bank account or issued as a check. The next several paragraphs describe how to deal with these debit cards if you are using the PouchPlan spreadsheet.

First, input the amount of the income into one

6-3: Manual Entry of Other Income

Enter your other income as a deposit to your bank account during the week of the month it is received.

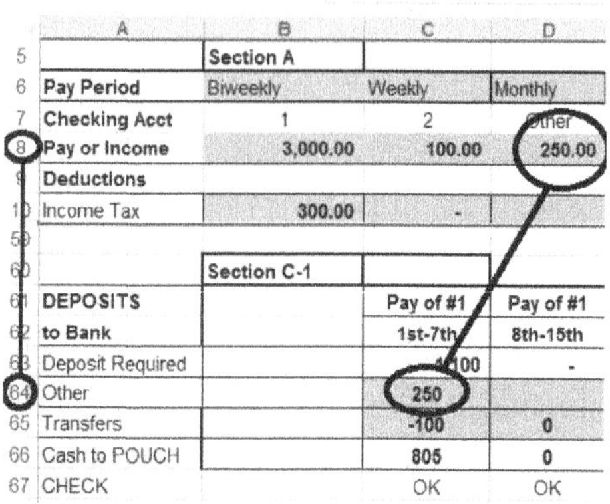

	A	B	C	D
5		Section A		
6	Pay Period	Biweekly	Weekly	Monthly
7	Checking Acct	1	2	Other
8	Pay or Income	3,000.00	100.00	250.00
9	Deductions			
10	Income Tax	300.00	-	
59				
60		Section C-1		
61	DEPOSITS		Pay of #1	Pay of #1
62	to Bank		1st-7th	8th-15th
63	Deposit Required		[illegible]	-
64	Other		250	
65	Transfers		-100	0
66	Cash to POUCH		805	0
67	CHECK		OK	OK

of the other income category columns in section A, Other income. That is all you have to do from the income side. On the expense side, you need to plan on spending the ENTIRE amount of the debit card on only one cash category

The other action you take is on the "Description" column in Section D on the bottom of the spreadsheet. Let's say that you have a child support debit card of $150 per month and a food and household budget of $750. You will put $600 of cash in the "Food and Household" pouch and also the $150 debit card for a total of $750. Yes, you actually put the card into the pouch category. When you make a purchase from that category, just whip out the card till it is all used up.

The debit card amount ($150 in the above example) will be listed on the "Debit/Credit" row (near the bottom on line 82) and not on a specific paycheck line. The spreadsheet will use the amount of the card

6-4: Debit or EBT Card as Other Income

EBT or debit card income will be moved directly to the pouch (Section D).

	A	B	C	D	E
1	**The Pouch**				
2	**Personal Budget Plan with Cash Timing**				
3	mwalker@PouchPlan.com				
4					
5		**Section A**			
6	**Pay Period**	Biweekly	Weekly	Monthly	Monthly
7	**Checking Acct**	1	2	Other	Other
8	**Pay or Income**	3,000.00	100.00	250.00	150.00
9	**Deductions**				
10	Income Tax	300.00	-		
11	ss	180.00			
68					
69		**Section D**			
70	**CASH**	FOOD & HOUSE	GAS	MISC	CLOTHES
71	**BREAKOUTS**	750	260	253	210
72	**#1 ck week #1**	300	100	100	75
73	**#1 ck week #2**				
74	**#1 ck week #3**	300	160	135	100
75	**#1 ck week #4**				
76	**#2 ck week #1**			18	17
77	**#2 ck week #2**				
78	**#2 ck week #3**				
79	**#2 ck week #4**				
80	**5th Paychecks**				105
81	**3rd Paychecks**				
82	**Debit Card**	150			
83	OK = 0, +/- 3	0	0	0	0
84					

for making sure each and every paycheck instruction is correct. Examples of this entry are provided on the "Example" tab in the workbook and in the figure above (see Figure 6-4).

If you have used a projection for income, you are going to need to use a projection for taxes. Social Security is simple; use 7.65 percent of your gross. For income taxes and retirement deductions, use the same *percentage* amount as last year's for your gross income. The rest of your deductions are typically fixed amounts and not impacted by a change in your gross income.

If you make changes in your income projection, the percentage deductions will need to be reviewed as well.

Varying income has proven to me to be the most difficult area to nail down for a person's budget. I have seen people who simply cannot handle the process and are constantly in trouble. Of course, they all had one thing in common: They *overestimated* their income. If you do not fall into that trap, the results of a miscalculation (i.e., *underestimating* your income) will end up being a pleasant adjustment instead of a disaster.

CHAPTER 7

Types of Expenses

REGULAR EXPENSES

Your "Regular Expense" category is a real time saver when you use the PouchPlan. *Regular expenses* are those expenses that are paid at the same time each month and are the same amount, or very close to the same amount, each month. Most people find that regular expenses make up between 40 to 85 percent of all their spending. (**BTT**) *All regular expenses are to be paid out of your checking account by automatic draft or automatic bill pay.* Writing out a check should become very rare. The only money you are depositing into your checking account each paycheck is the amount to cover these regular expenses. Your checking account is changing from a place where you park your money while you decide where to spend it to a dedicated account for paying specific bills. You will love reconciling a bank statement that has no outstanding checks.

Some regular expenses will be easy for you to identify. For example, your rent, insurance, car payment, and any loans probably come to mind immediately. But don't stop there. (**BTT**). *You will be doing yourself a favor if you try to think outside the box when coming up with your regular expenses.* What about child care? Do you have a self-storage rental unit? Any club dues or subscriptions? We even set up our church contribution as a regular expense. You can easily set up a monthly payment to an individual through your bank, for example, your housekeeper, babysitter, or dog walker. Consider everything that is paid on a regular monthly basis. What is so nice about regular expenses with the PouchPlan is that you do not spend any mental energy on them. You just set it and forget it. I think I've written one mortgage check in the last eleven years!

ALMOST-REGULAR EXPENSES

These types of payments are usually set up as a draft on your account by the service provider. (**BTT**) *We allow a bit of fluctuation on amounts, especially with utilities, but we need to make sure we never get caught short.* To solve this issue, we took all of our utilities for one year (water, electrical, gas, phone, and trash removal) and divided the total by twelve for our monthly utility amount. We also looked at our highest monthly amount (August in Texas) and used it as the first month's expense for our utilities, then went back to the average for the rest of the year. This way, we had the funds in the account from month 1 and did not have to worry when the dog days of summer hit. You can also contact your utility provider and see if they offer an "average" monthly payment option. Many electrical companies do. Most cell phones are the same from month to month as are almost all internet and subscription TV providers. This saves you a stamp, an envelope, and the hassle of having to remember to pay.

Quarterly and other nonmonthly but regular interval payments should be included in the "Regular Payment" section. You will need to adjust the amount to deposit each paycheck to match the time available to fund the payment. For example, I have an annual car insurance policy that is set up for $240 per quarter payments. My monthly budget has $80 in regular expenses for car insurance. Every three months when the draft hits my account, the money is there. This saves me from thinking about it and also saves me $24 of installment fees charged on the monthly payment plan offered by my insurance company.

(**BTT**) *Using quarterly payments on life and car insurance is a great option even if you are paid weekly.* Four months out of the year, you will be receiving five weekly checks instead of four. You can set up your budget (without the quarterly expenses included) based on forty-eight weeks of pay and then use the fifth week's check to pay your quarterly installments. This takes a bit of math and understanding of the PouchPlan to make it work and is best used by those with at least a couple of months experience on the system.

FIRST-TIME EXPENSES

The best way to start is to begin with the largest bill you pay each month and work your way down to the smallest. Your last two or three months' bank statements will be very helpful. (**BTT**) *Try to download your banking activity of three months into an excel spreadsheet. After the download, use the sort capabilities of excel to arrange the payments by amount, from largest to smallest. You should be able to quickly spot multiple payments of the same amount. These will become your regular payments.* Keep this sheet as it may also help you when you time your regular payments. If you cannot use excel, get a couple of highlighters and go through your bank statements marking off expenses until you have reviewed the entire statement. Again, start with the largest and move toward the smallest.

ADD A CUSHION

When we started out on the PouchPlan, "every dollar was assigned a specific duty." This is the classic and best way to start if you have never budgeted before. You need to know where every dollar is supposed to go as you try to identify opportunities for improving your budget and ultimately your bank account. Once you start to feel comfortable with the budgeting process and it becomes your habit, you can begin to build a little safety cushion in your bank account. I can clearly remember how good it felt when we started adding just $10 to our account per month. No longer was my balance going all the way down to $7.38 between paychecks. All I did was increase the estimate of our utilities to make the PouchPlan spreadsheet fund the cushion. We now add $25 per month to our utilities and end up taking a weekend trip or two to play with our grandkids when the extra money builds up enough.

CREDIT CARDS

This was a challenging area for us when we first started the PouchPlan. We purchase a lot of items online because we live in a fairly rural area. Obviously, you can't pay cash at the time of purchase and must use a credit card. I do not think it is wise to use a debit card tied to a bank account for online purchases. **(BTT)** *We started a separate category in our pouch labeled "Online."* Whenever we purchased items online, we use one specific credit card for all the purchases. At the same time the purchase is made, we moved cash from whichever category the purchase belonged into the "Online" category. Once a month, I would stop by the drive-through window of the bank and deposit the online cash in order to pay the credit card company.

All credit card companies give you the ability and option of paying online. If you use their website to handle the transaction, you will get a confirmation as soon as you authorize the payment. We later moved the "Online" category out of the pouch and into an envelope along with the credit card, which we keep in a drawer of our computer desk. Now when either of us goes online to make a purchase, everything is in one nice, tidy place. Yes, we formed a functional new habit.

SUMMARY OF REGULAR EXPENSES

1. Try to make as many of your expenses fit into your "Regular Expense" section as possible (set it and forget it!).
2. Start with your largest expenses and work your way down to the smallest ones as you set up your budget.
3. Group utilities and use the monthly average for the spreadsheet.
4. Keep your information regarding dates of regular payments as you will need it for the timing section.
5. Don't forget about the option of quarterly or semiannual payments.
6. And finally, build yourself a little cushion as it will make a nice place to sit when you hit a bumpy spot.

IRREGULAR EXPENSES

Irregular expenses are your expenses that are not paid on the same date or in the same amount from month to month. You will pay all of these expenses with cash from your pouch. You will create a separate pouch section for each category and will follow the instructions from the PouchPlan spreadsheet on how much to put into each category from every paycheck. Your irregular expenses are the easiest to change and are the first place you will look to if you need to make adjustments to your spending.

FIRST-TIME IRREGULAR EXPENSES

You are going to have to guesstimate when you first start. Irregular expenses are easy to tweak and move around. If you really don't have any idea of how much to put in a category, put in what you would like to spend on it. Start with the largest expenses and work your way down to the smallest. For most people, the largest expense will be "Food and Household" expenses. We combined the two categories into one after a couple of months because it was too much trouble to separate them out while standing in the Walmart checkout line!

(**BTT**) *You may have some regular expenses that you have to pay with cash as you start out on the PouchPlan.* We used a cleaning service that requested cash due to banking issues, and we started out by trying to remember to get cash from the account each week. I would forget more times than I remembered, so I moved the expense from the "Regular Expense" section to the "Irregular Expense" section. I moved it back to a regular expense and to an automatic bill pay when we changed service providers down the road.

You need to keep the number of irregular expense category items below ten. There are a lot of practical reasons for this limitation, but the main one is the spreadsheet is set up to handle a maximum of ten. As you list your expenses from the largest to the smallest, you may find that you have more than ten irregular expenses and need to combine several of the smaller ones. We combined our "Dry-Cleaning" category and our "Haircut" category into our "Looking-Good" category. It is OK if you have to combine more than two and label it your "Other" category.

Because anyone who has ever put together a PouchPlan has asked me, I am going to list a bunch of expenses that typically fall into the "Irregular" category. Don't worry if you don't have some, or even most, of these expenses. Just use this list to jumpstart your thinking about what you need to include in your plan to fit your life's activities and goals. So here is a list of the twenty most common expense categories (in random order) I have seen people put into their PouchPlan "Irregular Expense" section:

Food	Clothing	Gasoline
Gifts	School Activities	Learning Activities
Hair and Nails	Car Repair	Entertainment
Miscellaneous	Travel	Pet Care
Dry Cleaning	Yard Service	Maid Service
Child Care	Medical/Dental	Hobbies
Clubs	Adult Beverages	Household

"MISCELLANEOUS EXPENSES"

You absolutely have to have this category. You will never be able to identify every possible expense, and I do not want you wasting time and effort on what can be reduced to easy. I also use this category for expenses that only come once or twice a year. Christmas décor and spring gardening fall into this category. **(BTT)** *When you first set up a budget, this category needs to be about twice as big as you think is necessary.* I often have people put 50 percent of the amount of their largest irregular category as a starting point for "Miscellaneous." This will give you some room for error in your guesstimates without experiencing anxiety from the unknown.

Just last month, we used this category for car washes,

a couple of meals for a family whose mom had cancer, a new lamp for the bedroom, and contributions for the gathering of our family to celebrate our daughter and her family moving back to the area. If you have to cut expenses to balance your budget, try to cut other areas before you take from "Miscellaneous." This category has saved my rear end more times than I can remember.

ADJUSTING YOUR POUCHPLAN

Making changes to your irregular categories are easy and expected. All you do is move cash from one pouch category to another. The beauty is twofold: The system is always self-balancing, and you see the consequences of your decision in real time. Don't be hard on yourself. If expenses are higher in a category for the month than planned, just make the best choice for you and your family and move on. The PouchPlan is designed to serve you, not for you to serve it.

After a couple pay periods, you may notice a category or two that always needs extra funding. It is now time to make adjustments that are more lasting. Talk through the situation with the others who will be impacted by this decision. With the spreadsheet in front of you, you have a powerful tool to guide you in the discussion without blame or accusation taking over. Just stick to the facts and keep asking each other which spending adds to the goals and quality of life you are trying to achieve.

The options of how you make these adjustments are almost unlimited. In fact, if you have nine irregular categories and one needs to be increased, there are

512 possible combinations of reductions to the other categories you can put into play; for example, reduce some spending from all categories, take all needed funds from one category, reduce some spending from several categories, or delete all spending from several categories. Work toward the solution that provides the most gain with the least pain. If someone else is involved in the plan, remember that two brains always provide more knowledge, experiences, wisdom, and viewpoints than one.

Once you have decided that the change is going to be ongoing, and you have determined what categories need to be adjusted, it is time to change the spreadsheet. Do not change the spreadsheet for minor adjustments during the month. (**BTT**) *Be sure to print a hard copy of your current budget BEFORE you start to make changes or save the current budget on your computer.* (**BTT**) *Make all your changes at one time, and make them effective for the first pay period in the new month.*

SUMMARY OF IRREGULAR EXPENSES

1. Limit irregular categories to ten or less.
2. Start with the largest and work your way down to the smallest.
3. Combine the smaller categories to limit the overall number.
4. Make sure to include a "Miscellaneous" category.
5. Make small and temporary adjustments on the fly by moving cash between categories as needed.

6. Make all your permanent changes to the first pay period of the month.
7. Make a copy of your current plan (either a printed-out hard copy or save a copy on your computer) before you start to change the spreadsheet.

CHAPTER 8

Timing Expenses and the Cash Hierarchy

TIMING EXPENSES

Don't let the word *hierarchy* scare you; it just means arranging things in the order of their importance to you. The PouchPlan is able to give you specific instructions by paycheck because you tell the spreadsheet when each of your regular expenses needs to be paid during the month. This information is entered in section B-3, just to the right of where you have entered the descriptions and amounts of your regular payments. Section B-3 divides the month into four weekly periods and has columns for a 5th check if you are paid weekly and a 3rd check if you are paid biweekly. The only time you will use the 3rd or 5th-check columns of section B-3 is if you are paid weekly or biweekly. (**BTT**) *It is easier to begin this timing activity by entering all expenses into one of the four weekly periods and then deciding which ones fit best into the 5th or 3rd-check columns.* (See Figure 8-1.)

8-1: Regular Expense Periods

	A	B	C	D	E	F	G	H	I	J
1	**The Pouch**									
2	**Personal Budget Plan with Cash Timing**								Summary	OK
25										
26	**Section B-2**				Check # 1	**Section B - 3**				
27	Regular in frequency & amount					Week of the month				
28	**Spent from Checking**			Comment	**1st-7th**	**8th-15th**	**16th-23rd**	**24th-31st**	**5TH CK**	**3RD CK**
29	Paid from Checking # 1		Amount		Amount	Amount	Amount	Amount	Amount	Amount
30	Mortgage/Rent		800		800					
31	Tithe		650			300		300		300
32	Car Payment		250				250			

(**BTT**) *Arrange your regular expenses from the largest to the smallest, and then move across the page to enter the same amount on the same line under the column heading that matches which week of the month the payment is due. Column L is the proof or check column and will display a "0" when you have successfully entered the timing of each expense (see Figure 8-2). When all the regular expenses have timing entries that are correct, the box in cell L29 will display "OK."* If you do not have an "OK" displayed, you should look down column L to

8-2: Timing Entry Check

Column L showing all entries for timing of expenses made correctly.

	A	B	C	D	E	F	G	H	I	J	K	L
1	**The Pouch**											
2	**Personal Budget Plan with Cash Timing**								Summary	OK	0	
25												
26	**Section B-2**				Check # 1	**Section B - 3**						
27	Regular in frequency & amount					Week of the month						
28	**Spent from Checking**			Comment	**1st-7th**	**8th-15th**	**16th-23rd**	**24th-31st**	**5TH CK**	**3RD CK**		CHECK
29	Paid from Checking # 1		Amount		Amount	Amount	Amount	Amount	Amount	Amount	**Total**	OK
30	Mortgage/Rent		800		800						800	0
31	Tithe		650			300		300		300	650	0
32	Car Payment		250				250				250	0
33	House Insurance		150							900	150	0
34	Life Insurance		25							150	25	0
35	Cable		80				80				80	0
36	Internet		50							300	50	0
37	Electricty		200				200				200	0
38											-	0

see which line does not show a "0." Keep working on this until you get the OK in cell L29. The spreadsheet will now take over and move these amounts to the necessary areas.

TIMING OTHER INCOME

If you have other income, you need to read this entire subsection. The other income amounts from section A are not moved automatically by the spreadsheet like your paychecks are. If you have other income, you will need to enter that income on line 64 in the column that matches what week of the month you receive the income (see Figure 8-3). Lots of users group several types of other income together in section A, but here you will need to break those out if you receive them in different pay periods of the month. (**BTT**) *You need to have as many of these set up on direct deposit as possible. Or, you can hold them all and deposit them together at the end of the month.* I do not like to make trips to the bank,

8-3: Other Income From Section A

Enter your other income as a deposit to your bank account during the week of the month it is received.

	A	B	C	D
5		Section A		
6	Pay Period	Biweekly	Weekly	Monthly
7	Checking Acct	1	2	Other
8	Pay or Income	3,000.00	100.00	250.00
9	Deductions			
10	Income Tax	300.00	-	
59				
60		Section C-1		
61	DEPOSITS		Pay of #1	Pay of #1
62	to Bank		1st-7th	8th-15th
63	Deposit Required		1,100	-
64	Other		250	
65	Transfers		-100	0
66	Cash to POUCH		805	0
67	CHECK		OK	OK

so I put on the spreadsheet all my nondirect deposit other income as arriving on the last pay period of the month. If I get it in the bank earlier, that is fine, but as long as I'm not counting on it until later, I'm safe.

TIMING BANK DEPOSITS

The spreadsheet is going to automatically add together all of your expenses that are payable by each paycheck. This information is then displayed in section C on line 63 (see Figure 8-4). The amount needed to pay your regular expenses is then subtracted from your net check, and the difference is the amount of cash available for your pouch and is displayed on line 66, "Cash to Pouch" (see Figure 8-5). (**BTT**) *It is very common to have a negative amount show up on line 66, and this cannot be allowed. To do so would mean that you have not left enough in your bank account to pay all your bills that are due on that paycheck. Every number on line 66 must be 0 or higher.* As I said, it is not uncommon for this to happen, so let's look at what to do if you have this issue.

If the negative number on line 66 is not in the first pay period, you can move an expense (or part of an expense) into an earlier pay period than when it

8-4: Bank Deposits Required

Displays deposit amount required per paycheck to pay your regular expenses.

59							
60		Section C-1					
61	DEPOSITS		Pay of #1	Pay of #1	Pay of #1	Pay of #1	Pay of #1
62	to Bank		1st-7th	8th-15th	16th-23rd	24th-31st	5TH/3RD
63	Deposit Required		1,100	-	830	-	1,650
64	Other		250				
65	Transfers		-100	0	-80	0	0
66	Cash to POUCH		805	0	845	0	105
67	CHECK		OK	OK	OK	OK	OK

8-5: Cash to Pouch

Displays amount of cash available for pouch per paycheck.

59							
60		Section C-1					
61	DEPOSITS		Pay of #1	Pay of #1	Pay of #1	Pay of #1	Pay of #1
62	to Bank		1st-7th	8th-15th	16th-23rd	24th-31st	5TH/3RD
63	Deposit Required		1,100	-	830	-	1,650
64	Other		250				
65	Transfers		-100	0	-80	0	0
66	Cash to POUCH		805	0	845	0	105
67	CHECK		OK	OK	OK	OK	OK

is actually due. For example, your house payment is due on the 18th of the month and it is $800. If Line 66 shows a -$400 in the period from the 16 th-24th, you can move $400 of your house payment expense in section B-3 from the 3rd week of the month into either the 1st or 2nd week of the month. You would do this by changing the amount in the 3rd week of section B-3 to $400, and then enter the other $400 of your housing expense into one of the other earlier weeks. You will need to make sure line 66 shows all 0s and above as you make these moves. As long as you are moving an expense from a pay period later in the month to earlier, this will work. (See Figure 8-6.)

8-6: Moving Expenses Between Pay Periods

Example of splitting up mortage/rent into multiple pay periods.

	A	B	C	D	E	F	G	H	I	J	K	L
1	The Pouch											
2	Personal Budget Plan with Cash Timing								Summary	OK	0	
25												
26	Section B-2				Check # 1	Section B - 3						
27	Regular in frequency & amount					Week of the month						
28	Spent from Checking			Comment	1st-7th	8th-15th	16th-23rd	24th-31st	5TH CK	3RD CK		CHECK
29	Paid from Checking # 1		Amount		Amount	Amount	Amount	Amount	Amount	Amount	Total	OK
30	Mortgage/Rent		800		400		400				800	0
31	Tithe		650			300		300		300	650	0
32	Car Payment		250		200		50				250	0
33	House Insurance		150							900	150	0
59												
60		Section C-1						Section C-2				
61	DEPOSITS		Pay of #1	Pay of #1	Pay of #1	Pay of #1	Pay of #1	Pay of #2	Pay of #2	Pay of #2	Pay of #2	Pay of #2
62	to Bank		1st-7th	8th-15th	16th-23rd	24th-31st	5TH/3RD	1st-7th	8th-15th	16th-23rd	24th-31st	5TH/3RD
63	Deposit Required		1,100	-	830	-	1,650	150	90	60	180	100
64	Other		250							0		
65	Transfers		-100	0	-80	0	0	100	0	0	80	0
66	Cash to POUCH		805	0	845	0	105	50	10	40	0	0
67	CHECK		OK	OK	OK	OK	OK	OK	OK	OK	OK	OK

If the negative number on line 66 is in the first pay period or can't be moved up in the month, you are going to have to do one of two things: The first thing is to ask the vendor to move the due date. This is often very easy for them to do, especially if you are only needing a couple of days. I had one user get his mortgage company to change his due date by agreeing to pay twice monthly instead of only once. This also cut the total interest charged over the life of the loan. (**BTT**) *You should usually look at the largest bills to make changes like this, but when you are looking at asking for a change in a payment date, concentrate on those expenses that come due very close to the next pay period.* One user found out he had a seven-day grace period on a loan payment, and he only needed four days to get his cash to pouch line 66 in balance. He changed the drafting date at the bank and never did receive a negative response from the loan officer.

The other option is to "prefund" the expense in the prior month. In this example, we will say the house payment is due on the first day of the month, and it is still $800, and line 66 is showing the same -$400. You are going to have to move it to the last pay period of the PREVIOUS month and let the balance carry over in your bank account. This is only difficult to do the first month you use the PouchPlan. Beginning with month 2, you will already have prefunded the short amount owed during month 1. Month 2 will prefund month 3, month 3 will prefund month 4, and so on, without you making any other adjustments.

This area can be the most difficult part of your PouchPlan if you have several nonpayroll sources of income. Slow down, take a breather if necessary, and then take a bit of time to understand how much you have accomplished by getting to this point. Constantly refer to the proof or check parts of the spreadsheet. They will help keep you moving forward. You can also send me an e-mail at mwalker@pouchplan.com with a specific question. I will reply and usually add the question and answer to the "FAQ" section on the website. Seriously, you've made it 95 percent of the way. Don't give up now.

TRANSFERS BETWEEN ACCOUNTS

Before the advancements in electronic banking, we found out pretty quickly that two checking accounts were better than a shared one. It could have been my forgetfulness that prompted the separation, but it also makes a lot of sense from a control standpoint. The PouchPlan is set up to handle two checking accounts. You do not have to have two accounts if you don't want to; you can use one account and leave the other areas of the spreadsheet blank and it will function perfectly. (**BTT**) *If you choose to have two accounts, you pick up some flexibility because you can transfer funds between the accounts. If the two accounts are at the same bank, it becomes very easy.*

The ease of transferring funds comes in handy when you find the amount on line 66 is negative in one account and the other has plenty of funds to cover the shortage. In order to use this line, you need to enter the amount coming out of the checking account as a negative number, such as -$100. Then you need to enter the amount going into the other checking account as a positive number. Pay attention to the time frame of each transfer, as they need to be in the same pay period. Actually, you can transfer funds earlier than necessary, but you will end up in trouble if you transfer them later than needed. The example shows two transfers, one of $100 and one of $80, both are coming out of the same account and going into the other account. (See Figure 8-7.)

8-7: Transfers Between Accounts

Transfers are entered as a negative from the account being taken from and a positive into the account they are moving to.

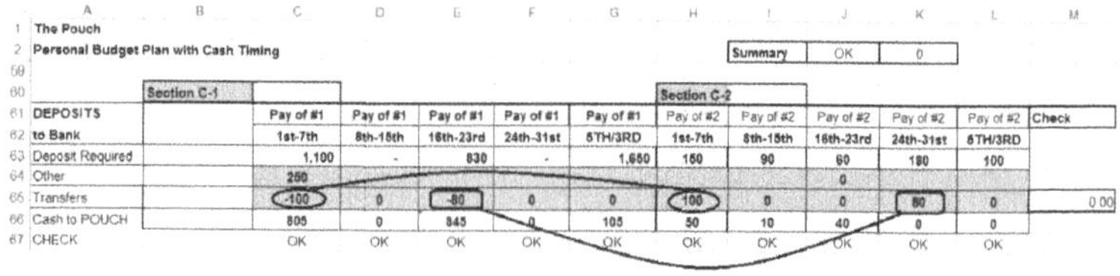

	A	B	C	D	E	F	G	H	I	J	K	L	M
1	The Pouch												
2	Personal Budget Plan with Cash Timing								Summary	OK	0		
59													
60		Section C-1						Section C-2					
61	DEPOSITS		Pay of #1	Pay of #1	Pay of #1	Pay of #1	Pay of #1	Pay of #2	Pay of #2	Pay of #2	Pay of #2	Pay of #2	Check
62	to Bank		1st-7th	8th-15th	16th-23rd	24th-31st	5TH/3RD	1st-7th	8th-15th	16th-23rd	24th-31st	5TH/3RD	
63	Deposit Required		1,100	-	830	-	1,650	150	90	60	180	100	
64	Other		250							0			
65	Transfers		-100	0	-80	0	0	100	0	0	80	0	0.00
66	Cash to POUCH		805	0	845	0	105	50	10	40	0	0	
67	CHECK		OK	OK	OK	OK	OK	OK	OK	OK	OK	OK	

(**BTT**) *It is a lot simpler to move money than to change a due date or prefund an expense.* You should set the transfer to take place automatically each month and then don't worry about it. OK, go ahead and check on it the first couple of months; it's really cool when it shows up. You can have money move both ways and multiple times during a month. You may need to check with your bank to make sure there is no charge for these transfers. Some types of accounts, savings accounts for example, limit your withdrawals per quarter based on FDIC rules. Just make sure whatever account the money is coming from has a negative number, and the one receiving the money gets a positive one on line 65.

THE CASH HIERARCHY

You are now in section D and you are almost done! All you have left is the decision of how much of the cash available from each paycheck goes into the individual sections of your pouch. In other words, if you have $500 cash available from a paycheck, this section is where you determine how that $500 is split among your irregular expenses. This is mostly common sense. You need food and you need toilet paper. If you run out of either of these things, it's a bad day. Really, that is all there is to this section. Even if you royally mess it up, you can still move money from one pouch section to another. So, let me walk you through the mechanics of section D.

Section D adds your entries both across the page and up and down the page. The addition going across the page makes sure the amount of each paycheck is totally distributed into the various pouch categories. The addition going down the page makes sure the various pouch categories get the correct amount of funding you set up in section B-1, your "Irregular Expenses."

The descriptions and amounts you put into section B-1 have automatically been filled in on lines 70 and 71. If you organized the expenses in section B-1 from highest to lowest, that same structure will be now displayed from left to right. Column M shows you how much cash you have to use from each paycheck to spread among your categories. You can get a good idea of what is happening if you will change the amount of one expense on line 72 and watch the change be displayed in Column M. The paycheck periods are listed on the left-hand side of the section. This first set of instructions, which will be the base set for all payroll periods, are all you need to master if you have monthly or semimonthly pay periods. I will give you additional instructions to handle weekly and biweekly pay periods in a couple of paragraphs. (See Figure 8-8.)

8-8: *Irregular Expenses Moved to Pouch*

Display of irregular expenses being automatically entered into Section D.

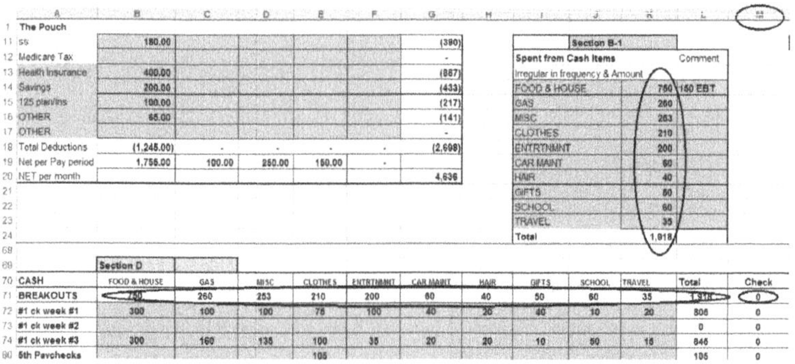

	A	B	C	D	E	F	G
1	The Pouch						
11	SS	180.00					(390)
12	Medicare Tax						-
13	Health Insurance	400.00					(867)
14	Savings	200.00					(433)
15	125 plan/ins	100.00					(217)
16	OTHER	65.00					(141)
17	OTHER						-
18	Total Deductions	(1,245.00)	-	-	-	-	(2,698)
19	Net per Pay period	1,755.00	100.00	250.00	150.00	-	
20	NET per month						4,636

Section B-1		
Spent from Cash Items		Comment
Irregular in frequency & Amount		
FOOD & HOUSE	750	150 EBT
GAS	260	
MISC	263	
CLOTHES	210	
ENTRTNMNT	200	
CAR MAINT	60	
HAIR	40	
GIFTS	50	
SCHOOL	60	
TRAVEL	35	
Total	1,918	

		Section D											
70	CASH	FOOD & HOUSE	GAS	MISC	CLOTHES	ENTRTNMNT	CAR MAINT	HAIR	GIFTS	SCHOOL	TRAVEL	Total	Check
71	BREAKOUTS	750	260	253	210	200	60	40	50	60	35	1,918	0
72	#1 ck week #1	300	100	100	75	100	40	20	40	10	20	805	0
73	#1 ck week #2											0	0
74	#1 ck week #3	300	160	135	100	35	20	20	10	50	15	845	0
80	5th Paychecks				105							105	0

MONTHLY AND SEMIMONTHLY PAY PERIODS

(**BTT**) *Start with the first paycheck that has cash available for the pouch. Begin entering the amount of cash you want to put in the first category in column B. The paycheck periods are in column A, on the left-hand side of the spreadsheet (see Figure 8-9). Stay on the same line and move to the right and decide how much you want to put into this category based on your spending needs. Repeat this same process until the amount in column M shows a 0. Column M goes down as you assign your available cash to each category.* Once you have a 0 in column M, go back and see if the amounts you put into each category make sense to you.

8-9: Cash Breakout of Paycheck

Dividing cash available from paycheck among your pouch categories.

	A	B	C	D	E	F	G	H	I	J	K	L	M
1	The Pouch												
68													
69		Section D											
70	CASH	FOOD & HOUSE	GAS	MISC	CLOTHES	ENTRTNMNT	CAR MAINT	HAIR	GIFTS	SCHOOL	TRAVEL	Total	Check
71	BREAKOUTS	750	260	253	210	200	60	40	50	60	35	1,918	0
72	#1 ck week #1	300	100	100	75	100	40	20	40	10	20	805	0
73	#1 ck week #2											0	0
74	#1 ck week #3	300	160	135	100	35	20	20	10	50	15	845	0
80	5th Paychecks				105							105	0
81	3rd Paychecks											0	0
82	Debit Card	150										150	
83	OK = 0, +/- 3	0	0	0	0	0	0	0	0	0	0		0

As you review your choices, try to compare how much you are contributing to a category to how much time you have between pay periods. Unless you are paid monthly, rarely will you have to fund an entire month's expenses for a category out of one pay period. Spread out your cash in ways that match how you best think you will need to spend it.

Now look down the bottom of the page to line 83. This line shows you how much cash you still have to allocate for each one of the individual irregular expense categories. (See Figure 8-10.) (**BTT**). *I found it easiest to work this line from left to right, reducing toward 0 the expenses on the left with the next available cash. Even if you do not take a specific expense all the way to 0, you should make sure it is adequately funded to handle the expenses that will come due before your next paycheck.*

8-10: Cash Funding of Pouch Categories

Pouch category correctly funded from paychecks and other incomes.

	A	B	C	D	E	F	G	H	I	J	K	L	M
1	The Pouch												
68													
69		Section D											
70	CASH	FOOD & HOUSE	GAS	MISC	CLOTHES	ENTRTNMNT	CAR MAINT	HAIR	GIFTS	SCHOOL	TRAVEL	Total	Check
71	BREAKOUTS	750	260	253	210	200	60	40	50	60	35	1,918	0
72	#1 ck week #1	300	100	100	75	100	40	20	40	10	20	805	0
73	#1 ck week #2											0	0
74	#1 ck week #3	300	160	135	100	35	20	20	10	50	15	845	0
80	5th Paychecks				105							105	0
81	3rd Paychecks											0	0
82	Debit Card	150										150	
83	OK = 0, +/- 3	0	0	0	0	0	0	0	0	0	0		0

I find it a lot easier to move around entertainment and clothing spending than I do gasoline and gifts. Therefore, I fund gasoline and gifts before I fund entertainment and clothing. It may take you a bit of experience to gain this type of insight, but it will come. In the meantime, do not worry. You can always move cash from one section to another during the month. (**BTT**) *My wife came up with a great way to keep track of moving cash between categories. Take the receipt and write on it the category from which you actually took the money to pay for the item and put the receipt in the category where you should have taken the money from. The next time you fund your pouch, the receipt will remind you of the IOU from the one category to the other.*

To recap: Don't move down a line until the paycheck period line you are working on shows a 0 in the checked column M. Take the expense columns down to 0 on line 83 in a right-to-left approach as well. Your last paycheck period will be a simple fill-in-what's-left exercise.

WEEKLY AND BIWEEKLY PAY PERIODS—3RD AND 5TH PAYCHECKS

Weekly paychecks result in four months during the year in which you will receive five paychecks instead of four. The PouchPlan spreadsheet identifies these as "5th Checks." When you set up your regular payments, we suggested you use these fifth checks to pay quarterly expenses such as insurance. If you were unable to do so, you will now need to consider which of your irregular expenses can handle being funded every ninety days. (**BTT**) *If there is not a category you feel can withstand* *the gaps in funding, you should spread this long-interval funding out among several different categories.*

Biweekly paychecks result in two months of the year in which you receive three paychecks instead of two. The best way of handling these real-long-gap income items is to assign them to pay for long-gap-expense items. Typically, house and car insurance payments are available in six-month terms, as are several other insurance types. Another option is to use them to prepay a monthly expense by just leaving the money in the account and not worrying about it. We did this with our satellite TV provider at one point. If you have to put some of this income into the "Irregular Expense" payments, try to use those expense categories where you have a great amount of control over when the actual expenses are to take place. Clothes and hair care would be an example of such expenses, where car repair and medical expenses can show up at anytime without warning.

When you enter an expense or the funding of your cash pouch into a 3rd or 5th-week cell, the spreadsheet automatically converts from the gross amount to the reduced amount that matches how big the gap was between checks. For example, the spreadsheet takes your gross $100 5th-week check and turns it into $33 for a monthly amount. For a $300, 3rd Biweekly check, the PouchPlan spreads that over six months at $50.00 per month. The spreadsheet does the same conversion for expenses. Due to this conversion by the PouchPlan, all you need to do is enter the **gross amounts** coming from each of your 3rd or 5th checks. (See Figure 8-11.) (**BTT**) *You can always make a copy of your spreadsheet to play with. When you do so, use nice round figures like*

$100 or $1000 as you experiment. This will help you to see and follow the math much easier.

When you have successfully achieved 0s down column M and 0s across on line 83, you have moved to the head of the class. Actually, you have. You have something 95 percent of your fellow planet dwellers do not have—a written and reviewed plan for your finances. I've seen it become an unbelievably powerful tool in my life and in the lives of others who got this far. Over the next thirty, sixty, and ninety days, the PouchPlan will become your habit. As it does, your life is going to get easier and better. Welcome to the move from "ouch" to "pouch"!

8-11: 5th and 3rd Check Examples

$300 third check amount is used to pay six months of internet at $50 per month. $90 fifth check amount is used to pay three months of car insurance at $30 per month. The PouchPlan spreadsheet makes these calculations automatically from the gross amount of these third and fifth paychecks.

	A	B	C	D	E	F	G	H	I	J	K	L
1	The Pouch											
2	Personal Budget Plan with Cash Timing								Summary	OK	0	
25												
26	Section B-2				Check # 1	Section B - 3						
27	Regular in frequency & amount					Week of the month						
28	Spent from Checking			Comment	1st-7th	8th-15th	16th-23rd	24th-31st	5TH CK	3RD CK		CHECK
29	Paid from Checking # 1		Amount		Amount	Amount	Amount	Amount	Amount	Amount	Total	OK
30	Mortgage/Rent		800		400		400				800	0
31	Tithe		650			300		300		300	650	0
32	Car Payment		250		200		50				250	0
33	House Insurance		150	semiannual						900	150	0
34	Life Insurance		25	semiannual						150	25	0
35	Cable		80				80				80	0
36	Internet		50	semiannual						300	50	0
37	Electricty		200		200						200	0
38											-	0
45	Total		2,205		800	300	530	300	-	1,650	3,855	0
46												
47	Section B-2.1				Check #2	Section B - 3.1						
48	Spent from Checking			Comment	1st-7th	8th-15th	16th-23rd	24th-31st	5th Chk	3rd Chk		CHECK
49	Paid from Checking #2				Amount	Amount	Amount	Amount	Amount	Amount	Total	OK
50	Tithe		43		10	10	10	10	10	0	43	0
51	School lunches		200		50	50	50	50			200	0
52	Phone		180		90			90			180	0
53	Electricty										-	0
54	Water & Trash		60			30		30			60	0
55	Car Insurance		30	quarterly					90		30	0
56											-	0
57											-	0
58	Total		513		150	90	60	180	100	0	513	0

CHAPTER 9

Balancing Your Budget: "Have To, Need To, Want To"

Remember how I said even a poor plan put into action will beat no plan every time? Please realize there is no reason to have a poor plan! I've already covered the basics you need to create a plan, but in this chapter, I'm going to share with you the best strategies I learned over my career that will double or even triple the worth of your planning. In each strategy we cover, I will walk you through the step-by-step tactics you will use to put your strategy into action. Remember that in your first attempt at the PouchPlan, all you are trying to do is to identify your spending needs and get to zero. Once you have that basic strategy down, it may be time to look at some additional options and strategies.

First, let me share a working definition of the two

words *strategy* and *tactics.* A *strategy* is like the fabric of an umbrella. When put into place, it provides a function and outcome that were desired. A *tactic* is like the rods or wires of the umbrella. They support and help the strategy produce the desired results. OK, so your goal is to stay dry in the rain. Your strategy could be to have a raincoat and hat; park your car in the handicap parking (even if you do not have a handicap sticker) and run real fast; wait the rain out in your car; use an umbrella; or just stay home. All of these strategies could keep you dry. (OK, the park and run is really an example of no plan!) Any one of these could be the best strategy to use depending on your situation.

After looking at all the possible strategies, you decide the umbrella is the best fit for your situation. Next come the tactics. Do you need a great big umbrella that covers two people? Do you need an umbrella that fits under the seat in your car? Do you need more than one umbrella? Once again, after considering your situation, you decide you need three umbrellas—one to leave at your place of work, one to leave in your car, and one to leave inside your home. You have a goal (to stay dry in the rain); a strategy (use an umbrella); and tactics to do so (three umbrellas at different locations). For as little as $30 and thirty minutes of time, you will stay dry from the rain and suffer as little disruption as possible to your real life.

One more major concept you need to understand: One size does not fit all. In the example above, the umbrella would have been a poor choice if you were a deckhand on an Alaskan fishing boat. And staying home may be by far the best choice if you have an illness that could be worsened by getting wet. The same philosophy applies to your financial situation and which strategy you use. Some of you will be deep in debt and can't even see the top of the hole you are in. Some will be just starting out and your income seems meager. Some may be getting married, and the challenge of sharing money issues with another person is new. Some of you may have nice incomes, but the stress and chaos in your life is painful. Some may have a working plan but now discover the simplicity of the PouchPlan will allow you to accomplish your goals with a better tool.

USE SEPARATE BUCKETS

When you are faced with needing to make changes in your expenses to balance your budget, where do you start? Here is where. Put each one of your budgeted expenses into one of these three buckets: Have To, Need To, and Want To. You make sure the Have To bucket is funded and each expense is reasonable; you question if the Need To bucket is important and contributing to your overall values and goals; you cut the dog out of the Want To bucket first.

Have To is just what it says it is. You "have to" buy this item or pay this bill or the consequences are bad and usually come quickly. If you don't pay your rent or your utilities, you will be on the street or without heat and water fast. If you don't make your car payment or keep your car insurance paid up, you will lose your car or have a ticket that is much more costly than paying the insurance bill. You "have to" eat and you "have to" bathe. (Hopefully, I don't have to tell you why.) If you don't have gas money for your car, you cannot go to work. The cost for not funding the Have Tos is a miserable life, and you can rest assured you will not be able to do the Need Tos or the Want Tos if you don't take care of the Have Tos first. Set these up to be paid automatically before you even get your hands on your money.

Need To is the area of expenses that adds value, peace, and freedom to your life. It reinforces your values and goals you have decided are important. You "need to" put aside money for car repair, but you might put it off for a week in order to fund a Have To expense. You "need to" dress appropriately for your job. You "need to" have an emergency fund. You "need to" provide educational and social growth opportunities for your children. Your spouse "needs to" know he or she is important in your life. You "need to" rest in order to restore your body and soul. You "need to" fund emergency and retirement needs. These things take funds and should be next in line after Have To.

Want To. Yes, this gets cut to the bone if necessary. But here is the good news that I have seen played out time and again. If you first take care of funding the Have Tos and the Need Tos on a consistent basis, it will not be long before you can begin to fund more of the Want Tos in your life. Please read that sentence again: *If you want more Want Tos in your life, the best way to get it is to make sure the Have To and Need To buckets are taken care of first.*

Following are four strategies I have successfully used to help move a plan from a good plan to a great plan. Each of these strategies has its strength and its struggles. I will describe both of those as I introduce each strategy. As I wrote this chapter, it dawned on me that I had used each of these strategies in our PouchPlan at different times over the last twenty-five years. I'm now using the simplest as we move toward the end of our earning years. We will start with the easiest and simplest strategy and move down the list to the most aggressive.

STRATEGY #1: THE PERCENTAGE STRATEGY

The Percentage Strategy is very effective because it is simple and doable. If this is your first time doing any budgeting or planning and you are not facing immediate financial stress, it is a great place to start. I have discovered of late it is also a great place to land after many years of meeting life's financial challenges. You divide major areas into a percentage that equals 100. A simple example is 10 + 10 + 80 for a three-area plan.

Once you determine your overall percentages, you then divide up the expenses within each area based on the amounts available. If you need to make changes in your Percentage Strategy, you are able to see the cost to the other areas that you previously decided were important. This allows you to make continual progress toward your overall financial goals because of the boundaries you have set.

The Percentage Strategy starts with determining your net take-home pay and dividing it into the major areas that will produce a balanced and prosperous financial future for you and your family. These areas are: #1 Savings, #2 Giving, and #3 Living. Oh, yes. You mess up the order and you will mess up your life. Actually, there are different and valid opinions on moving around the first two, but if number 3 does not remain number 3 on the list, this strategy will fail you. Period; end of story; get-off-the-planet type of failing. The reason is because you need to make a clear and understood value-driven choice about how much of your earnings belong in the first two areas and then the remainder becomes number 3. And yes, I remember that I said even a poor plan will beat no plan. In this case that is still true, but if number 3, Living, moves up, it's just barely better than no plan at all.

Experience has taught me if you set up more than four areas to fund, you might as well not use this strategy because you will reduce its major benefit of simplicity. I have found only two categories lacking but much better than none. The four-option strategy has you break your "Commitments" out into a separate budgeted area, and "Living" moves down to spot number 4. I like this four-option plan, but it does take a bit more math to set up.

The first key to making this strategy effective is to fund your areas based on their ranking. As one bucket fills up, funds become available for the next. The second key is to have that funding happen without any action on your part. Make sure the money from each paycheck is automatically set up to be moved out of your checking account and into the tool you are using to accomplish meeting each area's goal. If the money does not flow through your hands, you will not have to depend on your willpower to do what you already decided you wanted to do. The third key is that all adjustments are made first to the "Living" area, then to the "Savings" or "Giving" areas.

I've seen people use this strategy very effectively to fund college, weddings, and to get out of debt by setting up a percentage of their income that will automatically be moved to another account to fund this need or desire. You should spend some time deciding on the percentages that match your values and needs. Once you have made a clear choice, you will be better prepared to make your adjustments within the "Living" area only.

Here is an example of the math and real numbers from a couple who decided they wanted to "Live" on 75 percent, "Save" 10 percent, "Pay Down Debt" 10 percent, and "Give" 5 percent. Their take-home pay was $2,800 twice per month. So, on the first of the month, 10 percent or $280 went into a savings account, 10 percent or $280 was paid on existing debt above their regular payments, $140 or 5 percent was paid by draft to their church, and $2,100 was left in their account for living expenses in the first half of the month. This exact same process was repeated on the 15th of the month when they received their second paychecks.

The couple above adopted this aggressive budget after reading Dave Ramsey's book, *The Total Money Makeover*. It is a great book, and I highly recommend you get a copy. They wanted to get out of debt and used his "snowball" debt-reduction plan to accomplish that goal. Whenever they paid off one debt, the amount of that payment was added to the payment on the next debt they were paying off. For example, when their student loan of $210 was paid off, they would add that $210 to their car payment of $380 and send the bank $590 each month. They projected they would pay off all their debt, including an $180,000 home mortgage, in only seven years. Their motivation? How about a savings of $82,000 in interest on just their home loan alone.

STRATEGY #2: THE KAIZEN STRATEGY

Kaizen is the Japanese term for continuous improvement and was noticed by American manufacturers in the 1960-70s as Japan became more competitive after being decimated in WW II. The strengths of Kaizen as a budget strategy are that the results are cumulative (they stack one on top of another), and the changes are usually so small that our brains fit them into our current habits without noticing them. The downside is if you need to make major changes quickly, you may not have time for this powerful strategy to take effect.

I love the math of the Kaizen strategy. Really, I love it. Just think about this. If I could increase my income by just one-fourth of a percent each day, or 0.25%, my daily income would increase by 91.25 percent, almost doubling, in only one year. And this does not include any work or improvements on the weekends! Obviously, if it were that simple, everyone would be doing it, right? Here is a little secret. Those who never stop the "improvement" process are those who see the biggest gains.

To use Kaizen as a strategy, you implement every "improvement" that comes to mind no matter the size. You also take no category off the table for "improvement." One user found out that if she used a debit card with her bank account, the bank would waive the $2.95 per-month fee. She also found out that if she set up her car insurance on monthly drafts from the bank rather than sending in a check, the insurance company reduced the installment fee by $3.00 per payment. Now on a roll, she checked out everyone she paid each month to see if she could get a discount for bank drafts. While not all would give a discount, she figured she saved almost $300 in real money each year (worth more than three months of free gasoline) and a couple of hours per month in running around paying bills.

Kaizen says I will take the smallest step available today and tomorrow I will do the same. Can you refinance your mortgage for lower payments and not increase the mortgage term while lowering the rate? You won't know until you check it out. Does your insurance cost less if purchased on a quarterly, semi-annual, or annual basis? Does your newspaper cost less if you subscribe to their online version? Can you save on your cell phone if you change (or even threaten to change) carriers? What about your cable or satellite TV? Wow, let's just have a Kaizen party with our friends and see what ideas and options are out there. Best idea gets dinner paid for by everyone else!

There are two other attributes the Kaizen Strategy delivers that are worth mentioning: First is the "Low Fruit" picking that takes place when you start the process. I can guarantee you that a big ole blob of savings is going to fall right into your lap. According to the You Need a Budget website, the average person who gets on a budget finds $300 per month almost immediately. I've personally seen a couple "find" over

$1,100 per month in savings after just two weeks on the PouchPlan. Another family found $800. It will happen to you, too. The only unknown is how much you will find.

Second is the "Quantum Leap" or *tipping point phenomenon*. You will experience this when all the small actions add up to a monumental moment. An amazing point is when you have saved enough money to meet life's storms and have them pass by as though they were a sunny day. The classic is when you pay off all your debt, your entire life changes, and you are completely free to make your choices without having to consider meeting your financial commitments. Although I'm not there yet, I am really excited about the day my assets produce more income than I choose to live on—day after day, one-quarter of 1 percent. You gotta love that math program.

STRATEGY #3: THE BRIDGE-BUDGET STRATEGY

The Bridge Strategy is great for examining your entire budget in an organized and efficient manner. It gives you most of the advantages of a zero-based budget without all the hassle. (FYI, a zero-based budget is one where you justify and list every expense you plan on incurring.) Zero-based budgets consume vast amounts of resources, time, and expertise to produce. In my experience, you get 85 percent benefits with only 10 percent of the effort when you use the Bridge Strategy. The downside of the Bridge Strategy is that you must have an established budget to compare it against. This does not mean that you can't use it as your first PouchPlan budget, just that you will need some budget for comparison in order to use this strategy. This is an excellent budgeting tool to use with excel or other spreadsheet apps.

Start the Bridge with 5 columns and as many rows as you have expense categories. Once again, include your regular and irregular expenses. Column 1 is for your description; column 2 is for your current budget numbers; column 3 is for the changes you want to make; column 4 is for the new budget amount; and column 5 is for your comments and notes. (See Figure 9-1.)

9-1: Bridge Budget Example

Template takes Column B "Current Amount" plus (+) or minus (-) Column C "Change" to equal Column D "New Budget Amount".

	A	B	C	D	E
1	**Bridge Budget Template**				
2					
3	**Expense Description**	**Current $**	**Change $**	**New $**	**Comments**
4					
5	Expense 1	100	-25	75	
6	Expense 2	100	-15	85	
7	Expense 3			0	
8	Expense 4			0	
24	Expense 20			0	
25	Expense 21			0	
26	Total	200	-40	160	

The math works like this: Column 2 +/- Column 3 = Column 4. In English, it sounds like this: Current budget plus or minus changes equals new budget amount with comments in column 5. The key to making this a real effective strategy is the question, "What did I like and not like about the results of this spending during the last budget?" This is a very results-focused way of examining your old and therefore your new budget. This question is also why the strategy can consume a considerable amount of time and effort.

If you decide to use the Bridge Strategy, I would suggest that the first time you go down the list you look for the obvious and you look for waste. What categories do you feel with your gut are out of proportion? Which ones have an uncomfortable feeling or leave a bit of a sour taste every time you think about them? A lot of times, you can cut these categories down without much effort. I paid for a ministorage unit for fifteen years and only went to it three times during that period. What a waste! I obviously did not need any of that stuff. The Bridge Strategy forced me to decide if cleaning it out was worth the $35 per month, or $415 per year. (Actually, $415 x 15 = $6,225 over fifteen years. Definitely worth the day it required setting up the Bridge Strategy!)

As you go down the list the second time, begin to make decisions based on the importance of each category in comparison to the other categories. I hate to pick on the "Hair" area again, but is it possible to postpone the time in between visits by one week? If you were going once a month, can you survive once every five weeks? You would then have ten visits during the year versus twelve in the previous plan. If your visits cost $50, you made a $100 change to your budget with limited pain (except in my house where my back would be hurting from sleeping on the couch).

Where the 80/20 Strategy that we discuss next almost always involves major changes, the Bridge Strategy lets you pick and choose with more consideration of the downside of the changes. The Bridge Strategy also has more of an improvement attitude rather than just survival at its core. It is a great exercise to do once a year, whether you need to cut your budget or not.

STRATEGY #4: THE 80/20 BUDGET STRATEGY

The principle that a minority of your actions produces a majority of your results refers to 80/20. The math may be 70/30 or 95/5. The exact math is not critical. What you must come to understand is that just a few actions will produce the majority of the results you are after. This strategy is very effective if you are in massive financial trouble or you know the financial cliff is just around the corner because it can produce huge changes very quickly. The negative part is that 80/20 often requires the biggest and most painful changes to your lifestyle. The need for this strategy becomes obvious after you have put together your first budget and can clearly see there is no way out unless big changes are made.

Begin your 80/20 budget by listing ALL of your expenses, starting with the highest and moving down to the lowest. You should be able to use your PouchPlan spreadsheet to help you identify and rank your expenses. Be sure and include your cash expenditures in your rankings as well as your regular payments. Now start adding them together as you go down the list until you have reached a total of your expenditures that equals between 70 and 80 percent of your total expenses. You will probably be surprised how few expenses it takes to make up this 80 percent number. These are the first expenses you need to concentrate on reducing.

The bad news is I can tell you what is most likely going to be in this 80 percent number—your house payment and your car payment and other things you like that are expensive. You will also find that "Food and Household" is often in the 80 percent. But here is the good news. When you take the brave step to address the big-spending items, the smaller-spending items tend to decrease on their own. Look at the example of the downsizing of a home. When the cost of a home goes down, so does the insurance and taxes. If the new home is actually smaller in size, you should also see a reduction in utilities and upkeep. The same principle applies to cars.

You continue down your 80 percent list and get rid of all questionable spending. Have a vacation home, boat, RV, or other plaything that has a payment? You need to be ruthless. None of this is fun, but the quicker you stop the bleeding, the quicker the healing can begin. The healing will come…and usually very soon.

The 80/20 Strategy is also an excellent tool to use to examine if your spending choices align with your values and goals. It is very easy to let unwanted expenses creep into your spending habits if you do not examine their alignment every so often. We once realized that our "Children's Activities'" budget was getting larger and larger. We already knew the entire family was stressed and maxed out with our schedules. My sweet wife came up with a great idea. Everyone could pick one activity at a time, but only one. If you wanted to dance, dance. But you could not do gymnastics at the same time. If you wanted to play baseball, then soccer would have to wait while they overlapped. This had some impact on our budget, but it sure made our lives much less stressful and demanding.

BONUS STRATEGIES

Bonus Strategy #1 is to combine the parts you like best from the above strategies as you gain experience. Build a foundation of a budget that you understand and then add to it as you grow in your expertise. If you think something will add to the effectiveness of your strategy, give it a try. Keep it if it does and throw it out if it doesn't. This approach has a lot of positives; the only negative is if you make your strategy too confusing, then the odds of your continuing the plan will drop considerably.

Bonus Strategy #2 is to use no pouch in the PouchPlan. In this strategy, you set up all your regular expenses in your checking account, and you open another, second checking account for your irregular expenses. All your irregular expenses are included in one category—the second checking account. You pay your irregular expenses from this account with either a debit card, check, or cash. The strength of this strategy is that you limit cash transactions and it is really simple.

If you use the 80/20 Percentage Strategy to identify your regular expenses, you can make solid progress toward financial goals with Bonus Strategy #2. The negatives are that you will not be able to identify low-hanging savings and you can find yourself low on irregular money as the month progresses due to "expense creep." I have seen this work for folks who could not get the entire PouchPlan up and running successfully. It is much better than no plan and could be a serious option if this is your first time to ever budget.

Bonus Strategy #3 is to use a debit card from a separate checking account for the largest of your irregular expenses. We did this for our "Food and Household" category when it was running $600 to $700 per month because we did not want to carry that much cash around. When using this tactic, you place the debit card instead of cash in the pouch section. You can easily check the balance of your account by phone, so it requires very little effort to determine how much you have available to spend.

Which strategy is right for you? It depends on your situation. I will tell you that if you are new to budgeting or have tried before and not been able to make it work, you should pick the strategy that makes the most sense to you and go with it. Don't worry about not having all the pluses of all the strategies. If you put any of these into effect, it will produce excellent results. After four to six months of experience, come back and reread this chapter. You will spot opportunities you could not have fully appreciated your first time through, and you will be glad you did.

CHAPTER 10

Tips, Shortcuts, and Best Practices

The top three questions that always seem to come up when I introduce people to the PouchPlan are:

1. Isn't it risky to carry around so much cash?
2. What is a typical budget for people in my income range?
3. What's the best way to increase my income?

The truth is these are great questions and show a high degree of involvement by those who asked them. So let me share with you what twenty-five years of PouchPlan use, along with stints at corporate America and multiple entrepreneurships, have taught me.

SAFETY AND RISK

Carrying cash does expose you to more risk than not carrying it. Therefore, it is right to take some steps to lower that risk. The very best way to reduce this risk is to reduce the number of expenses you have to pay with cash. If you can set up the majority of your bills as regular payments, you can reduce the amount of cash you're carrying around tremendously. We have found that many pouch users can approach 80 percent of their total spending as regular payments and then pay those bills by electronic payments. Using electronic payments is a massive win for you. It will reduce the time, cost, hassle, and risk all at the same time.

The number one risk of carrying cash is that of accidental loss due to forgetfulness. People have taken the pouch out to pay for something, got distracted, and forgot to put it back into its safe carrying place. Sometimes this doesn't end badly, but a lot of times it does.

The next most common loss was caused by some kind of incident in the home. This might include a puppy getting the pouch and using it as a teething toy or children using the pouch to play "store" with. Although we have never had any user experience it, you should consider the possibility of a fire if you are building up a significant quantity of cash in your pouch.

The least common but most feared loss is the loss by theft. And yes, if you are going to carry around cash, you will need to be more observant and careful by paying attention to your surroundings and taking some commonsense actions. Just because you know you are carrying cash does not mean anyone else knows, unless you tell them.

THE MINIPOUCH

An extremely effective risk reducer and useful tool is what we call the minipouch. My wife and I actually have three pouches—the main pouch and two minipouches. The main pouch is the one funded from each paycheck, and our two minipouches are funded with cash moved from the main pouch on an as-needed basis. For years, my wallet's credit card section with its four holders served as my minipouch. I would put $40 for "Food and Household," $40 for "Gasoline," and $20 each for "Miscellaneous" and "Entertainment" in my wallet, and it would last me at least a week, if not longer.

My wife would typically carry twice as much cash as I did because she handled most of the grocery, household, and clothes shopping. She would always have her minipouch in her purse and would take along the main pouch if she was planning some serious shopping that day. By splitting up the cash into two minipouches and taking the main pouch only when needed, you really reduce the exposure and risk of carrying cash.

REDUCING CASH RISK

My wife has a system she follows every time she makes a purchase, and I honestly don't know if she is even aware of it. She sets her purse on the checkout counter, and reaching in, she opens the pouch and takes the needed cash out of the correct category and hands it to the cashier. She waits for her change, puts it in the pouch, and puts her purse back on her arm. If I am with her and she has more than a handful of items, she hands me her purse. By following this routine, she hides the pouch's contents from other shoppers and prying eyes, never letting it out of her physical possession, and looks just like every other shopper in the store. The only consistent downside is that my shoes rarely match her purse.

I do not like to carry the pouch into a store unless I am wearing a jacket or coat. My pockets are not large enough for our main pouch to fit into comfortably. I also would never get out of my car to buy gas or something else at a convenience store with the pouch in my hand. In both of these instances, I will take enough cash from the pouch to make my purchase and put the cash in my front pocket. I then place the pouch in the glove box or console of my car, sometimes even under the front seat, but always completely out of view, lock my car, and go take care of business. When I return to my car, I retrieve the pouch and place the change in the proper section.

This is important to remember: If there is nothing of value within view, the chances of someone breaking into your car are almost zero. So do not leave the pouch in a purse in the front seat or in a laptop case with a phone showing in the backseat. If you don't attract them, they will not come.

Around the home, there are several easy fixes that take almost no effort or cost: First, especially if you have children, have a designated drawer, cabinet, or at least a landing spot that is out of the way where the main pouch "lives" when not in use. This also helps if you use minipouches so one spouse is not always asking, "Where is the pouch?" It doesn't have to be in the root cellar behind last year's rutabaga crop, but it should not be on the end table next to the front door, either. A bedroom dresser is always a winner for this choice.

Taking care of the fire risk is even easier. Both your refrigerator and freezer offer prime spots for fire protection and theft reduction. Unless there is an explosion or the building burns for hours without being put out, these appliances survive most house fires with the contents pretty much intact. There are several types of containers available that mimic common brand packages designed to store your cash. We do not even bother with that much deception. We just used a small Tupperware container and put it next to the Blue Bell homemade vanilla ice cream in the freezer. (I guess this is where the term "cold cash" comes from.) We used this trick several times as the pouch got "fat" from saving up for back-to-school shopping with five kids.

Don't forget to consider option 2 in the Bonus Strategies section of the previous chapter. That strategy removes the cash risk from the budgeting process, but you lose some other very nice benefits.

SAMPLE BUDGETS

First, let me make a huge disclaimer. These budgets "exactly" fit about 4 out of the 330,000,000 people who currently call the United States of America their home. For our international readers, that means about 80 of the 8 billion people on earth are going to need no changes in these budgets. The rest of you should consider these just as guides—good guides—but still guides nevertheless. I'm going to show four budgets—two for singles and two for families. The singles' budgets will be for annual incomes of $25,000 and $50,000 (see Table 10-1), and the families' budgets will be for annual incomes of $36,000 and $72,000 (see Table 10-2). I will show percentage ranges as well as actual dollars and will use the middle of the percentage for the dollar amounts. If you have a currency other than the US dollar, you can use the percentage and your local currency and the budgets will still be valid. Of course, you should consider variation in cost of living and local peculiarities no matter where you live.

These examples, as well as several other useful tools, are available for free on my website at www.PouchPlan.com when you download the free PouchPlan spreadsheet. I have also not included charitable giving on these samples. That is an extremely personal decision, and although my wife and I are tithers to our church, this book is not designed to cover the subject in much detail. I will say our giving is one of the most satisfying ways we get to spend our money. Our PouchPlan budget includes our giving in the top section right before the tax line.

Table 10-1. Sample Budgets for Singles

Single $25,000				**Single $50,000**			
Monthly Income	**$**	**2,085**	**100%**	**Monthly Income**	**$**	**4,165**	**100%**
Taxes	$	(175)	-8.4%	Taxes	$	(500)	-12.0%
Health Ins	$	(210)	-10.1%	Health Ins	$	(270)	-6.5%
Retirement	$	(50)	-2.4%	Retirement	$	(250)	-6.0%
Savings	$	(75)	-3.6%	Savings	$	(250)	-6.0%
Net Take Home	$	1,575	75.5%	Net Take Home	$	2,895	69.5%
House payment/Rent	$	500	24.0%	House payment/Rent	$	900	21.7%
Food & Household	$	240	11.5%	Food & Household	$	300	7.2%
Car Payment	$	200	9.6%	Car Payment	$	380	9.1%
Utilities	$	130	6.2%	Utilities	$	170	4.1%
Other/Miscellaneous	$	100	4.8%	Other/Miscellaneous	$	285	6.8%
Clothes	$	75	3.6%	Clothes	$	150	3.6%
House & Car Insurance	$	60	2.9%	House & Car Insurance	$	110	2.6%
Gasoline	$	60	2.9%	Gasoline	$	100	2.4%
Cell Phone	$	50	2.4%	Cell Phone	$	100	2.4%
Activities/Entertainment	$	50	2.4%	Activities/Entertainment	$	150	3.6%
TV/Internet	$	50	2.4%	TV/Internet	$	100	2.4%
Gifts	$	30	1.4%	Gifts	$	100	2.4%
Car Maintenance	$	30	1.4%	Car Maintenance	$	50	1.2%
	$	1,575	75.5%		$	2,895	69.5%

The next set of sample budgets are for families. Again the disclaimer, but this time it is even more important: No two families are exactly alike. I assumed two parents and two children as I developed the sample budgets. This may not even be close to your actual family makeup and that is OK. This is a give-and-take exercise and a guide to start you on the path to your values and plan. This is to help you if you do not know where to start. So start here and go where your dreams and desires lead you.

Table 10.2 Sample Budgets for Families

Family $36,000			Family $72,000		
Monthly Income	**$ 3,000**	**100%**	**Monthly Income**	**$ 6,000**	**100%**
Taxes	$ (200)	-6.7%	Taxes	$ (650)	-10.8%
Health Ins	$ (400)	-13.4%	Health Ins	$ (500)	-8.3%
Retirement	$ (100)	-3.3%	Retirement	$ (400)	-6.7%
Savings	$ (100)	-3.3%	Savings	$ (400)	-6.7%
Net Take Home	$ 2,200	73.3%	Net Take Home	$ 4,050	67.5%
House payment/Rent	$ 700	23.3%	House payment/Rent	$ 1,250	20.8%
Food & Household	$ 400	13.3%	Food & Household	$ 700	11.7%
Car Payment	$ 300	10.0%	Car Payment	$ 600	10.0%
Utilities	$ 150	5.0%	Utilities	$ 245	4.1%
Other/Miscellaneous	$ 100	3.3%	Other/Miscellaneous	$ 200	3.3%
Clothes	$ 100	3.3%	Clothes	$ 200	3.3%
Gasoline	$ 100	3.3%	Gasoline	$ 180	3.0%
Activities/Entertainment	$ 80	2.8%	Activities/Entertainment	$ 200	3.3%
Cell Phone	$ 80	2.8%	Cell Phone	$ 150	2.5%
TV/Internet	$ 70	2.3%	TV/Internet	$ 100	1.7%
Gifts	$ 40	1.3%	Gifts	$ 60	1.0%
House & Car Insurance	$ 40	1.3%	House & Car Insurance	$ 100	1.7%
Car Maintenance	$ 40	1.3%	Car Maintenance	$ 65	1.1%
	$ 2,200	73.3%		$ 4,050	67.5%

I hope your income is more than the examples shown above. If that is the case, start by setting your expenses at the actual numbers in the higher budget and see if that level of spending makes sense to you. Try hard to keep the levels of savings and giving above 20 percent and you will be richly rewarded. After you have used these samples for guidance, return to the four strategies described earlier in the book and apply the one you like to your unique situation.

INCREASING YOUR INCOME

As we close out this chapter and the book, I want to share with you my advice and my answer to a question that usually comes up after PouchPlan users have made solid progress on controlling their expenses. At some point, even dedicated efforts start to produce diminishing results. This is the time to switch your focus to increasing your income. In all my years (forty-plus) dealing with businesses from a financial and management standpoint, I never saw one cut their way to prosperity. I saw plenty cut their way out of trouble and several stay competitive by cutting costs. The only ones that grew to prosperity were those that invested their resources to continually increase the value of their services or products to their customers.

The one product or service we can all increase the value of is ourselves. There are many things in life you cannot control, but you always have control over the choices you make. What have you done to make your value to others go up? What resources are you investing in yourself? Ben Franklin said this over 250 years ago: "If a man empties his pouch into his head, no man can take it away from him."

You will find plenty of places to start investing in yourself if you ask this question of just three people: "What can I do for you to be a better _____?" First, ask your spouse, or if single, your closest friend, and fill in the blank with the word *husband, wife*, or *friend*. Next, ask your boss or employer and fill in the blank with the word *employee*. And finally, ask yourself and change "you" to "me" and fill in the blank with your dream. You may shock people the first time you ask them this question, so be prepared to have to repeat it several times over a period of a couple of weeks. Don't give up; just be polite and persistent. This is a great way to invest in yourself without spending any money.

When you get an answer, repeat it back to them with the answer in a question. "So, if I spent some time talking to you about your day and my day before I turn on the television or start a project, I would be a better husband to you, right?" Or, "If I complete all my paperwork before I leave for the day that would increase my value to you as an employee, correct?" Then do it every day for the next week! Leave yourself sticky notes on your mirror, chair, and desk and plan your time to make sure it happens. After one week, ask if your performance or behavior has had the result the person you had asked had hoped for. If it has, just smile and say, "That's great" and continue the behavior for the next week. At the end of week 2, ask again if the behavior is continuing to have the hoped-for results. Again, just smile and say "great" and continue for week 3.

After three weeks, a couple of major things are going to have changed: You have a very positive new habit that has been formed in your major relationships, making them stronger. You have a new skill, the question and follow-through that you can repeat again and again. You should ask this question each month in any area where you want improvement in the value you deliver. Over one year, this will produce improvement in twelve specific actions that the person receiving the service or product has declared are valuable to him or her. Zig Ziglar was fond of saying, "You can get anything you want in life if you will just help enough other people get what they want." You will separate yourself from the 95 percent of mediocre folks real quick with this trait.

I left the question you ask yourself for last on purpose. It is the hardest to get an answer for, but if you keep asking it, you will get answers. Don't be afraid to invest some of your pouch in this quest. Do you know what your natural strengths and skills are? What kinds of challenges are easy for you to master, and what kinds are tough? How do you relate to certain types of personalities and forms of communications? You can get answers to all these and many more questions from several readily available and affordable testing services.

Finding out what drives you and what you are naturally gifted for will open up your eyes to all kinds of possibilities. It will also open up the path to greater income if you will focus on your strengths. I will leave you with this one very important point that aligns with the principle that you cannot cut your way to prosperity. Everyone, including you, will be better off and happier if you let those who excel in your areas of weakness assist you in those tasks. The development and improvement of your strengths are what will bring prosperity and purpose to your life. With the right plan and action, you can enjoy the ultimate "ouch" to "pouch."

BEST READS, WEBSITES, AND SOURCES

We are extremely fortunate to live in a time where knowledge is so easily and inexpensively available. You can locate expert advice in a matter of minutes with a smart phone or computer just by asking for help. The most successful people on the planet are available for you to learn from and to copy. There is also a bunch of bull out there that is just as easy to fall into, especially when it comes to money. I want to share with you some of the most helpful sources I've found in fifty years of searching. These resources cover a lot more than just advice on money. But you should have expected this range of sources as I have been continuously writing that money affects many parts of your life. You can also learn a lot about money by understanding the other parts of your life as well.

- *The Success Principles* by Jack Canfield—Best all-around read; takes a long time to digest it all.
- *Total Money Makeover* by Dave Ramsey—Great for reducing debt.
- *The Prosperous Soul* by Stephen De Silva—Exciting view of prosperity versus scarcity as a life viewpoint.
- *Money, Possessions, and Eternity* by Randy Alcorn—Interesting Christian view of money and things.
- *The Automatic Millionaire* by David Bach—A how-to manual with lots of real doable actions.
- *Think and Grow Rich* by Napoleon Hill—A classic, but still true.
- *How to Win Friends and Influence Others* by Dale Carnegie—Another classic that should be brought back.
- *Uncle Eric Book* series by Richard Maybury—May only be available at www.bluestockingpress.com but well worth the effort to find.
- *Intelligent Investor* by Ben Graham—Taught Warren Buffett; enough said.
- *The 80/20 Principle* by Richard Koch—Contemporary of Mitt Romney at Bain Capital and now on the leading edge of business thinking.

I also listen to and gobble up what a couple of people have to say. Perry Marshall is an 80/20 Guru who gets it better than just about anybody. Check out his website at www.Perrymarshall.com. Clark Howard has a radio show and has written several books. If there is a way to do it for less, this guy knows it. His website is www.clark.com. You also won't go wrong reading Ken Blanchard, Suze Orman, John Maxwell, Jim Collins, or Zig Ziegler.

If you are not reading the Bible, you are missing out on the most read book on the planet. It has stood the test of time as wisdom literature. The "new" part is almost two thousand years old. For a more intimate daily experience, *Jesus Calling* by Sarah Young is about as good as it gets. C S Lewis is a clear thinker and great storyteller.

I am not a financial advisor and the PouchPlan is not designed to be all you need to get to the finish line; it is what you will build your financial castle on. There are many professionally trained and expert people, from CPAs to CFPs, who you can seek out as your wealth and needs grow. You will need them sooner than you expect if you start your PouchPlan today.

CHAPTER 11

The PouchPlan Quick Start Guide

Welcome to the PouchPlan. You are about to embark on a very simple activity that has the power to change your life. You will end up with a spreadsheet that tells you how much cash goes into each pouch section from each and every paycheck—an automated deposit schedule matched against expenses and timed to NEVER miss a payment, incur a late fee, or allow an overdraft charge again. And…well, let me quote a recent user of the PouchPlan: "I never, ever thought I could have such control over my money. I believe I spend less time each paycheck on the PouchPlan than it takes me to make a peanut butter and jelly sandwich!" If you have not already done so, you can download a copy of the spreadsheet at www.PouchPlan.com for free. Your first time through should take between two and three hours. Some people will finish much quicker and a few will take a bit longer. After you have completed the plan, you will only spend a few minutes on it after you receive each paycheck. When you follow the instructions below, in a couple of hours or so, you will have a budget, an outline that times your expenses, a deposit schedule, and a funded POUCH that you can depend on to continue making financial progress from this day forward.

FIRST INSTRUCTION—SAVE A COPY OF THE MASTER SPREADSHEET. Name it MASTER copy. The PouchPlan allows you to make as many copies as you need for your personal use. I have probably saved fifty or more over the last twenty-five years. I use the following naming pattern: Pouch??? 01 01 17 (???= your initials, followed by day, month, year). Looks like this in real life: PouchMFW 01 01 17. When it is time to save your PouchPlan, you should name it to reflect whose it is and when it was made. So now save a copy with your naming information. This is the copy you will use as we move forward. Also, it is a good idea to print these instructions; most users find a hard copy easier to follow as they fill in the spreadsheet.

Just a quick word about Excel© and other common spreadsheets. You will be moving around the spreadsheet, entering both numbers and text. The instructions will refer to "cells" by an alphanumeric combination, such as "C8." You will need to identify which specific cell to go to in order to follow the instructions. Fortunately, this is solved by the spreadsheet labeling its columns (these run up and down the page) and its

11-1: Excel Labeling of Rows and Columns

Display of "Cell C8"

	A	B	C	D	E	F	G
1	**The Pouch**						
2	**Personal Budget Plan with Cash Timing**						
3	mfwalker1106@gmail.com						
4							
5		**Section A**					
6	**Pay Period**	Bi-Weekly	Weekly	Monthly	Monthly	Monthly	
7	**Checking Acct**	1	2	Other	Other	Other	Total
8	**Gross Pay**	**3,000.00**	**100.00**	**250.00**	**150.00**		**7,333**
9	**Deductions**						
10	Income Tax	**300.00**	-			-	**(650)**
11	ss	**180.00**					**(390)**
12	Medicare Tax						-
13	Health Insurance	**400.00**					**(867)**
14	Savings	**200.00**					**(433)**
15	125 plan/ins	**100.00**					**(217)**
16	OTHER	**65.00**					**(141)**
17	OTHER						-

rows (these run sideways across the page). Columns are labeled with letters starting with *A,* and rows are labeled with numbers beginning with 1. So cell "C8" is located in the 3rd column on the page and on the 8th row down the page (see Figure 11-1).

I prefer to use a mouse to move from cell to cell, but you can also use the arrows on your keypad. A left click on your mouse opens the cell for input. The shaded areas on the spreadsheet are the only areas that allow input (see Figure 11-2). The remainder of the cells are locked as they may contain formulas that automatically fill in parts of the spreadsheet as you input your information.

One other very helpful suggestion is to read these instructions as you follow along on the filled-in example(s) on the "Sample" tab (see Figure 11-3). This will give you real numbers to see and feel. I use the same numbers on the "Sample" tab spreadsheet that I use in the examples in this book. Users have responded that

11-2: Display of Shaded Areas

Only the shaded areas will allow user entry.

	A	B	C	D	E	F	G
1	**The Pouch**						
2	**Personal Budget Plan with Cash Timing**						
3	mfwalker1106@gmail.com						
4							
5		**Section A**					
6	**Pay Period**	Bi-Weekly	Weekly	Monthly	Monthly	Monthly	
7	**Checking Acct**	1	2	Other	Other	Other	Total
8	**Gross Pay**	3,000.00	100.00	250.00	150.00		7,333
9	**Deductions**						
10	Income Tax	300.00	-			-	(650)
11	ss	180.00					(390)
12	Medicare Tax						-
13	Health Insurance	400.00					(867)
14	Savings	200.00					(433)
15	125 plan/Ins	100.00					(217)
16	OTHER	65.00					(141)
17	OTHER						-

11-3: Display of Sample Worksheet Tab

25							
26	**Section B-2**			Check # 1	**Section B - 3**		
27	Regular in frequency & amount				Week of the month		
28	**Spent from Checking**		Comment	**1st-7th**	**8th-15th**	**16th-23rd**	**24th-31st**
29	Paid from Checking # 1	Amount		Amount	Amount	Amount	Amount
30	Mortgage/Rent	800		400		400	
31	Tithe	650			300		300
32	Car Payment	250		200		50	
33	House Insurance	150	**semiannual**				

Master | **Sample** | Future Value Deposits | Future value of amount | Bridge Budget

the total time required to complete the PouchPlan was the same whether they used the "Sample" tab or not, but the experience was more pleasant and less stressful for those who did a "practice" effort first.

INCOME – SECTION A

OK, let's do this. Open up the spreadsheet with your name on it and move your curser to cell B6. Left click on the mouse, and a drop-down box will appear with an arrow pointing down. Click on the arrow and the

11-4: Pay Period Drop-down Box

Click on the pay period to display arrow. Click on the arrow to see options and select pay period.

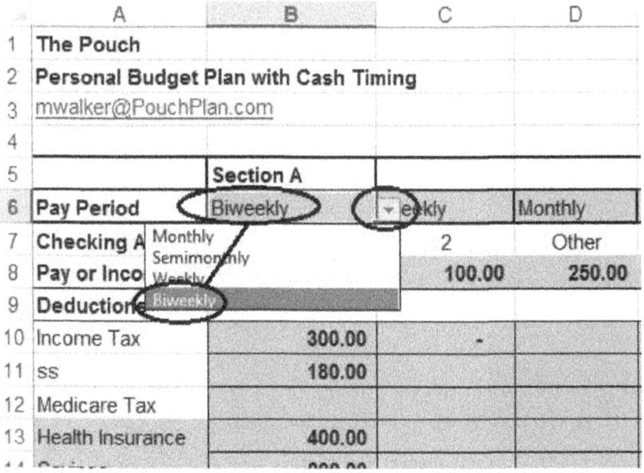

available choices appear. Drop-down boxes give you specific options to choose from. The options in this box match the frequency of your paycheck. There are four choices: Monthly, Semimonthly, Biweekly, and Weekly. Move the cursor over the correct one and left click. (See Figure 11-4.)

Get a copy of your paycheck or stub and input your pay data. You have two choices on how to enter your paycheck. You can either enter the Gross Pay or Take Home Pay. If you enter your Take Home Pay, you DO NOT enter any payroll deductions. This is the easiest and will work just fine for most users. If you chose Take Home Pay enter that amount in cell B8 and you are done for that check. Repeat the same process for a second check in cell C8.

If you chose Gross Pay, you will now enter your paycheck deductions. Begin in cell C8 and Input your Gross Pay (your pay BEFORE any deductions). Next, move down column B from B10 to B17, inputting each deduction from your paycheck. These are entered as positive numbers; the spreadsheet will subtract the total from your gross pay. Remember, you can change the labels on any cell that is shaded. If you have more deductions than cells, it is best to add the smaller ones together and enter that sum in B17. ***Excel tip***: *You can add, subtract, and do other math functions inside an excel cell. To do so, begin your math series with the = sign as the first entry in the cell, and then just put your parts together. Example: = 2+2 and the cell will display 4.* The amount in cell B19 needs to match the amount of your net or take home pay. If it does not, check the numbers on the spreadsheet and make sure they match your check stub until you get it to be the same net amount. If you have just one source of income, you are done and can move to section B, "Expenses." (See Figure 11-5.)

For those who have multiple sources of income, we are going to split that situation into two sets of instructions. If you have additional paychecks, the next two paragraphs will handle those options. If you have sources of other income, those instructions will take place after we cover multiple paychecks.

For the second paycheck, the first decision to be made is based on the frequency of the paycheck and if you are going to be using multiple checking accounts. If the second paycheck's frequency is the same as the first, the easiest thing to do is to use the excel math function and add the two amounts together in each cell in column B. In other words, add the gross

11-5: Comparison of Entering Gross and Take Home Pay

If entering take home pay, only enter the net amount of your paycheck on Row 8. If entering gross pay on Row 8, you must enter all deductions from each paycheck.

	A	B
1	The Pouch	
2	Personal Budget Plan with Cash Tir	
3	mfwalker1106@gmail.com	
4		
5		Section A
6	Pay Period	Bi-Weekly
7	Checking Acct	1
8	Pay or Income	1,755.00
9	Deductions	
10	Income Tax	
11	SS	
12	Medicare Tax	
13	Health Insurance	
14	Savings	
15	125 plan/Ins	
16	OTHER	
17	OTHER	
18	Total Deductions	-
19	Net per Pay period	1,755.00
20	NET per month	

Take Home Paycheck

	A	B
1	The Pouch	
2	Personal Budget Plan with Cash Tir	
3	mfwalker1106@gmail.com	
4		
5		Section A
6	Pay Period	Bi-Weekly
7	Checking Acct	1
8	Pay or Income	3,000.00
9	Deductions	
10	Income Tax	300.00
11	SS	180.00
12	Medicare Tax	
13	Health Insurance	400.00
14	Savings	200.00
15	125 plan/Ins	100.00
16	OTHER	65.00
17	OTHER	
18	Total Deductions	(1,245.00)
19	Net per Pay period	1,755.00
20	NET per month	

Gross Paycheck

pay amounts together in B8, and add the similar deductions together in each of cells B10 to B17. (See Figure 11-6.)

If the frequency of the second paycheck is different from the first, you will need to enter it as a new check in cell C6 and follow the instructions in the previous paragraph, changing the cells to column C in place of column B in the instructions. (See why I said you might want to print out these instructions!) You should also use the new paycheck option for paycheck #2 if you are planning on using two checking accounts. If you have more than two paychecks, you are going to have to

11-6: Combining Same Pay Period Paychecks

If the pay periods are the same, paychecks from different sources or individuals may be combined.

	A	B	C
1	**The Pouch**		
2	**Personal Budget Plan with Cash Timing**		
3	mfwalker1106@gmail.com		
4			
5		Section A	
6	**Pay Period**	Bi-Weekly	Bi-Weekly
7	**Checking Acct**	1	2
8	**Pay or Income**	2,000.00	1,000.00
9	**Deductions**		
10	Income Tax	200.00	100.00
11	ss	120.00	60.00
12	Medicare Tax		
13	Health Insurance	200.00	200.00
14	Savings	100.00	100.00
15	125 plan/ins	50.00	50.00
16	OTHER	45.00	20.00
17	OTHER		
18	Total Deductions	(715.00)	(530.00)
19	Net per Pay period	1,285.00	470.00
20	NET per month		

Same Payperiod but seperately listed paychecks

	A	B	C
1	**The Pouch**		
2	**Personal Budget Plan with Cash Timing**		
3	mfwalker1106@gmail.com		
4			
5		Section A	
6	**Pay Period**	Bi-Weekly	Bi-Weekly
7	**Checking Acct**	1	2
8	**Pay or Income**	3,000.00	-
9	**Deductions**		
10	Income Tax	300.00	-
11	ss	180.00	
12	Medicare Tax		
13	Health Insurance	400.00	
14	Savings	200.00	
15	125 plan/ins	100.00	
16	OTHER	65.00	
17	OTHER		
18	Total Deductions	(1,245.00)	-
19	Net per Pay period	1,755.00	-
20	NET per month		

Same Payperiod paychecks combined

combine them into the two available paycheck columns, B and C, using the excel math functions. Use the totals on row 19 to validate your entries. (See Figure 11-7.)

"Other Income" covers items such as child support, EBT, food stamps, rental, and interest and investment income. It is very important that we include all income in our budget. As we say about the PouchPlan, "Every Dollar has a Duty." We have given you three columns—D, E, and F—for listing other income (see Figure 11-8). These columns should be used to group other income according to how the funds are delivered to you. In other words, where does the money actually end up? For example: Child support directly deposited to your bank would go into a different column than food stamps on an EBT card. This is because the EBT card limits the types of items one can purchase, and the money never passes through your bank account.

11-7: Paychecks From Different Pay Periods

If paychecks have different pay periods they require separate entries.

	A	B	C
1	**The Pouch**		
2	**Personal Budget Plan with Cash Timing**		
3	mwalker@PouchPlan.com		
4			
5		Section A	
6	**Pay Period**	Bi-Weekly	Weekly
7	**Checking Acct**	1	2
8	**Pay or Income**	3,000.00	100.00
9	**Deductions**		
10	Income Tax	300.00	-
11	ss	180.00	
12	Medicare Tax		
13	Health Insurance	400.00	
14	Savings	200.00	
15	125 plan/Ins	100.00	
16	OTHER	65.00	
17	OTHER		
18	Total Deductions	(1,245.00)	-
19	Net per Pay period	1,755.00	100.00
20	NET per month		

11-8: Other Income Columns

5		Section A					
6	**Pay Period**	Bi-Weekly	Weekly	Monthly	Monthly	Weekly	
7	**Checking Acct**	1	2	Other	Other	Other	Total
8	**Pay or Income**	3,000.00	100.00	250.00	150.00		7,333
9	**Deductions**						
10	Income Tax	300.00	-			-	(650)
11	ss	180.00					(390)
12	Medicare Tax						-
13	Health Insurance	400.00					(867)
14	Savings	200.00					(433)
15	125 plan/Ins	100.00					(217)
16	OTHER	65.00					(141)
17	OTHER						-
18	Total Deductions	(1,245.00)	-	-	-	-	(2,698)
19	Net per Pay period	1,755.00	100.00	250.00	150.00	-	
20	NET per month						4,636

Interest income could be included with child support IF the child support was deposited into the checking account. Some states have child support deposited to debit cards, and those would need to be listed separately for our purposes.

Start with using the three provided columns, then combine other income amounts as needed per their common delivery method. Use "net" amounts for this income. Example: IRA distributions commonly have income tax withheld, so you would input the net amount after the tax deduction on the spreadsheet. This is a bit more difficult of an area for some folks, as the options are many. The good news is that once this is done, there are usually very few changes necessary for long periods of time.

11-9: Summary Box

This summary box shows a budget that is out of balance by $50 and a budget that is in balance.

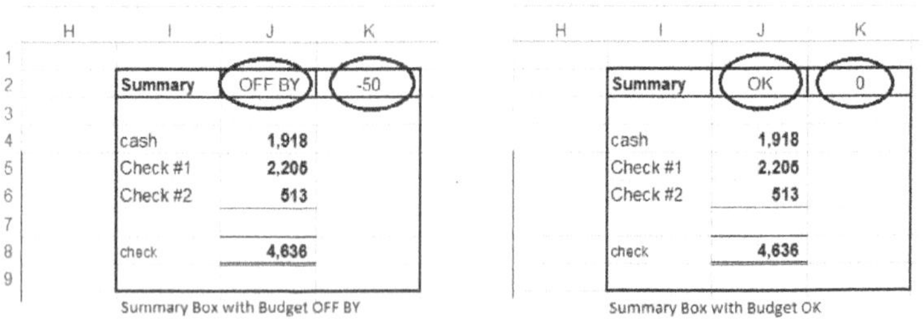

Summary Box with Budget OFF BY

Summary Box with Budget OK

Now is a good time to introduce you to the Summary Box; it is located beginning on column **I**, row 2 (see Figure 11-9). This box tracks your overall progress and lets you know if you have successfully planned for all income and expenses. Right now, the Summary Box should tell you that your budget is "OFF BY" the amount of your net income. You can watch your progress by checking the Summary Box at any time.

EXPENSES – SECTIONS B AND C

Regular Expenses

The PouchPlan has you divide your expenses into two categories, "Regular" and "Irregular." *Regular expenses* are those that are approximately the same in both frequency and amount. Regular expenses will be paid from your bank account. An example of a regular expense is the rent or mortgage payment. It is the same amount and is due the same date each month. Car payments, insurance, and cable TV are other examples of *regular* payments.

Irregular expenses are those expenses whose amount and timing fluctuate all the time. Irregular expenses will be paid with cash. An example of an irregular expense is entertainment. It rarely takes place at the same time each month, and the expense varies considerably based on the activity and other variables. Groceries, gifts, and gasoline are other examples of irregular expenses.

We are going to start with the "Regular Expenses," section B-2. Scroll down the spreadsheet to cell A30. Your checkbook and bank statement can be very helpful as you identify these types of expenses. Look for the largest expenses and start with those. This way if you miss one, you will miss a small one. Also, the most common regular expenses are listed for you in the shaded area, which you can easily change. Type the name of the expense in column A, then the amount in column C. If you have a comment to add, you can do so in column D. Take some time and make sure you have as many regular expenses as possible listed in this area. I like to include my utilities in this area as they are approximately the same each month, and I enter the average based on a yearly amount. If you have more expenses than lines, use the "add" function of excel and combine the smaller amounts in cell C44 (or on the last available line), and label it "Other." (See Figure 11-10.)

If you entered data for paycheck #2, you will need to divide up your expenses by which paycheck is to be used to pay which expenses. I would advise you to list all of your regular expenses in Section B-2 first, then divide them between the two income streams. Use section B2.1 to list which expenses are to be paid by

11-10: Regular Expenses Section B-2

Various regular expenses entered into Section B-2

	A	B	C	D
1	**The Pouch**			
2	**Personal Budget Plan with Cash Timing**			
3	mwalker@PouchPlan.com			
26	**Section B-2**			
27	Regular in frequency & amount			
28	**Spent from Checking**			Comment
29	Paid from Checking # 1		Amount	
30	Mortgage/Rent		**800**	
31	Tithe		**650**	
32	Car Payment		**250**	
33	House Insurance		**150**	**semiannual**
34	Life Insurance		**25**	**semiannual**
35	Cable		**80**	
36	Internet		**50**	**semiannual**
37	Electricty		**200**	
38				
39				
40				
41				
42				
43				
44	Other			
45	**Total**		**2,205**	

paycheck #2. Totals are displayed in cells C45 and C58 that you can use as a guide. An expense can be split between the two accounts. For example: Mortgage of $800 can be split as $400 and $400. (See Figure 11-11.)

When you have all your regular expenses determined, it is time to arrange them into time payment periods. Sections B-3 and B-3.1 are used to record the amount of the expenses into the time periods in which they occur. The headings in this section list six options. For semimonthly and monthly paychecks,

11-11: *Splitting a Single Expense Between Two Accounts*

An $800 mortgage/rent expense is split between two checking accounts.

3	mwalker@PouchPlan.com				
26	**Section B-2**			Check # 1	S
27	Regular in frequency & amount				V
28	**Spent from Checking**		Comment	**1st-7th**	
29	Paid from Checking # 1	Amount		Amount	
30	Mortgage/Rent	**400**	**Split**	**400**	
31	Tithe	**650**			
32	Car Payment	**250**		**200**	
33	House Insurance	**150**	**semiannual**		
34	Life Insurance	**25**	**semiannual**		
35	Cable	**80**			
36	Internet	**50**	**semiannual**		
37	Electricty	**200**		**200**	
44	Other				
45	**Total**	**1,805**		**800**	
46					
47	**Section B-2.1**			Check #2	S
48	**Spent from Checking**		Comment	**1st-7th**	
49	Paid from Checking #2			Amount	
50	Tithe	**43**		**10**	
51	School lunches	**200**		**50**	
52	Phone	**180**		**90**	
53	Mortgage/Rent	**400**	**Split**	**400**	
54	Water & Trash	**60**			
55	Car Insurance	**30**	**quarterly**		
56					
57					
58	**Total**	**913**		**550**	

this is a straightforward activity and is easily accomplished by entering the amounts of the expenses into columns E through J on the same lines as you earlier recorded each expense. Once column L shows all "0s" on each line, you are finished with this section. Make sure you show all "0s" in column L for sections B-3 and B-3.1. (See Figures 11-12.1 and 11-12.2.)

Weekly and biweekly pay periods start with the same method for the first four weekly time periods but will require an additional step. The "5th CK" and

11-12.1: *Regular Expenses Prior to Timing of Payments*

Column L displays amounts not entered for timing of your expense payments.

	A	C	D	E	F	G	H	I	J	K	L
1	**The Pouch**										
2	**Personal Budget Plan with Cash Timing**							**Summary**	OK	0	
3	mwalker@PouchPlan.com										
26	**Section B-2**			Check # 1	**Section B - 3**						
27	Regular in frequency & amount				Week of the month						
28	**Spent from Checking**		Comment	**1st-7th**	**8th-15th**	**16th-23rd**	**24th-31st**	**5TH CK**	**3RD CK**		**CHECK**
29	Paid from Checking # 1	Amount		Amount	Amount	Amount	Amount	Amount	Amount	**Total**	**OFF BY**
30	Mortgage/Rent	**400**	**Split**							-	-400
31	Tithe	**650**								-	-650
32	Car Payment	**250**								-	-250
33	House Insurance	**150**	**semiannual**							-	-150
34	Life Insurance	**25**	**semiannual**							-	-25
35	Cable	**80**								-	-80
36	Internet	**50**	**semiannual**							-	-50
37	Electricty	**200**								-	-200
44	Other									-	0
45	**Total**	1,805		-	-	-	-	-	-	-	-1,805

11-12.2: *Regular Expenses After Timing of Payments Entered Correctly*

Column L displays that all expenses have been correctly entered into the timing of your payments.

	A	C	D	E	F	G	H	I	J	K	L
1	**The Pouch**										
2	**Personal Budget Plan with Cash Timing**							**Summary**	OK	0	
3	mwalker@PouchPlan.com										
26	**Section B-2**			Check # 1	**Section B - 3**						
27	Regular in frequency & amount				Week of the month						
28	**Spent from Checking**		Comment	**1st-7th**	**8th-15th**	**16th-23rd**	**24th-31st**	**5TH CK**	**3RD CK**		**CHECK**
29	Paid from Checking # 1	Amount		Amount	Amount	Amount	Amount	Amount	Amount	**Total**	**OK**
30	Mortgage/Rent	**400**	**Split**	**400**						400	0
31	Tithe	**650**			**300**		**300**		**300**	650	0
32	Car Payment	**250**		**200**		**50**				250	0
33	House Insurance	**150**	**semiannual**						**900**	150	0
34	Life Insurance	**25**	**semiannual**						**150**	25	0
35	Cable	**80**				**80**				80	0
36	Internet	**50**	**semiannual**						**300**	50	0
37	Electricty	**200**		**200**						200	0
44	Other									-	0
45	**Total**	1,805		800	300	130	300	-	1,650	3,455	0

"3rd CK" columns (columns I and J) are only used if you have weekly or biweekly pay periods and refer to a "5th Weekly Check" or "3rd Biweekly Check" for the month. (See Figure 11-13.) This will happen four times per year for weekly paychecks and twice a year for biweekly paychecks. You are going to have to trust the spreadsheet to do its magic because this is not very intuitive for most people. Identify expenses that can be paid on either a quarterly or semiannual basis. The common ones are insurance, giving, and taxes.

If you are budgeting for either of these expenses, use the 5th & 3rd CK columns to list them. For example: Your car insurance is $60 a month or $180 a quarter or $360 semiannually. If you are paid weekly, you would put the quarterly amount of $180 on the car insurance line in the "5th CK" column (I), which is **three times the monthly amount**. If you are paid biweekly, you will put $360 in the "3rd CK" column (J),

11-13: Entry of 5th or 3rd Check into Section B-3, Timing of Expenses

The PouchPlan spreadsheet automatically calculates the monthly budget amount of 5th weekly or 3rd bi weekly checks. In the above example, the tithe of $300 is spread out for your budget into $50 per month over six months. The house insurance expense of $900 is also spread out over six months, at $150 per month, because it is also a 3rd check expense. The process is the same for 5th weekly checks, but the budget covers three months of the expense rather than six.

	A	B	C	D	E	F	G	H	I	J	K	L
1	**The Pouch**											
2	**Personal Budget Plan with Cash Timing**								**Summary**	OK	0	
3	rnwalker@PouchPlan.com											
26	**Section B-2**				Check # 1	**Section B - 3**						
27	Regular in frequency & amount					Week of the month						
28	**Spent from Checking**			Comment	**1st-7th**	**8th-15th**	**16th-23rd**	**24th-31st**	**5TH CK**	**3RD CK**		**CHECK**
29	Paid from Checking # 1		Amount		Amount	Amount	Amount	Amount	Amount	Amount	**Total**	OK
30	Mortgage/Rent		800	**Prepay 1/2**	400		400				800	0
31	Tithe		650			300		300		300	650	0
32	Car Payment		260		200		60				260	0
33	House Insurance		150	**semiannual**						900	150	0

which is **six times the monthly amount**. The PouchPlan spreadsheet automatically reduces this back to a monthly amount in column K. Try to use up as much of the 3rd/5th paycheck as you can with these types of expenses as it will help smooth out our next section. Use column L to make sure you have assigned all payments a payable date that balances out against the expenses with nothing but "0s" displayed in sections B-3 and B-3.1. (See Figures 11-14.)

11-14: 5th Check Adjustment by Spreadsheet

This shows the 5th check amount automatically covering three months of budgeted expense for car insurance.

	A	B	C	D	E	F	G	H	I	J	K	L
1	**The Pouch**											
2	**Personal Budget Plan with Cash Timing**								**Summary**	OK	0	
3	mwalker@PouchPlan.com											
46												
47	**Section B-2.1**				Check #2	**Section B - 3.1**						
48	**Spent from Checking**			Comment	**1st-7th**	**8th-15th**	**16th-23rd**	**24th-31st**	**5th Chk**	**3rd Chk**		**CHECK**
49	Paid from Checking #2				Amount	Amount	Amount	Amount	Amount	Amount	**Total**	**OK**
50	Tithe		43		10	10	10	10	10	0	43	0
51	School lunches		200		50	50	50	50			200	0
52	Phone		180		90			90			180	0
53	Mortgage/Rent										-	0
54	Water & Trash		60			30		30			60	0
55	Car Insurance		30	quarterly					90		30	0
56											-	0

Irregular Expenses

Your next step is to list those expenses that are NOT regular in amount or frequency, such as groceries, gasoline, clothing, household items, gifts, and so on. Go to section B-1 that begins on row 11 in column I. On you first run-through, you are going to probably need to be OK with some ballpark estimates on these types of expenses. Start with what you think you are currently spending, and we can and will adjust as required. These are monthly amounts, but it may be helpful to think weekly or per activity to decide on the monthly amount. For example, if $150 is the average you spend at the grocery store and you go once per week, that would equal $600 or so on "Food and Household" for your entry per month. Same with gas. You fill up your car 2-3 times per month, and it costs $50 per tank, so you should enter $100 to $150 on your "Gas" expense line. Remember, you can change any description that is in a shaded area to match your needs. (See Figure 11-15.)

The PouchPlan suggests you keep the total number of categories in this section to ten or less, with six to eight being ideal. It becomes burdensome to handle more, and the gain is not worth the pain. It is a good idea to combine small expenses into the category of "Miscellaneous" (and to put a little extra in it for good measure) if you find you have too many categories

11-15: Irregular Expense, Section B-1

Listing of some common irregular expenses and their amounts.

I	J	K	L
	Section B-1		
Spent from Cash Items			Comment
Irregular in Frequency & Amount			
FOOD & HOUSE		**750**	**150 EBT**
GAS		**260**	
MISC		**253**	
CLOTHES		**210**	
ENTRTNMNT		**200**	
CAR MAINT		**60**	
HAIR		**40**	
GIFTS		**50**	
SCHOOL		**60**	
TRAVEL		**35**	
Total		**1,918**	

of expenses. Enter all your irregular expenses, and then rearrange them to have the largest at the top of the list.

BALANCING YOUR PLAN

Time to check the "Summary Box." Odds are the summary will still be "OFF BY" some amount. If the amount is positive, meaning you have money left over in your account, you need to plan what to do with that amount and account for it on your spreadsheet. Remember, "Every Dollar has a Duty." If you cannot think of any other expenses you might have missed, a good choice would be to increase your savings and then wait and see if you missed an expense when you live out your plan. You can always reduce your savings amount and add the expense without much effort on your part. If you have a negative amount, which is much more common, meaning you have less money than you budgeted for, you are going to have to cut your expenses. You must get the "Summary Box" to display (0) in Cell K2.

Concentrate your efforts first on your "Irregular Expenses" as they are the easiest to adjust or cut. If you think about it, it is rarely easy to just increase your income. Your expenses in the "Regular" section are often difficult to adjust in the short term but may provide the largest change in amounts when they are actually made. This process can be a challenge, but this is where you really begin to take control of your financial foundation. The spreadsheet will help you identify any input errors by displaying problems in the "Check" areas in columns L or M. You are now telling

11-16: Summary Box

This summary box shows a budget that is out of balance by $50 and a budget that is in balance.

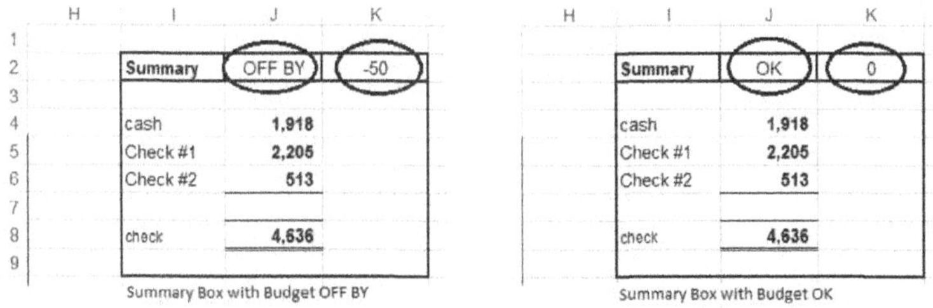

your money where to go and what to do. This is an awesome and powerful step. You must keep at it until the "Summary Box" displays "(0)." (See Figure 11-16.)

Success!

Congratulations! You have moved to the top of the class! I'm not kidding. Well over 90 percent of Americans have never been able to establish a plan for spending their income the way they want to. As a result, they live lives of fear and desperation, mired in debt, living from one paycheck to the next. That may describe your PAST, and you may not love the current picture, but you now have the information, the tool, and the power to literally change your financial FUTURE. You have one more section, "Cash Timing," to put the icing on the cake, but you have already completed the heavy lifting. Some PouchPlan users find it best to look over, review, and make adjustments to their plans for a few days before moving to the "Timing" section. However, the next section is where you put the program on autopilot and is crucial for long-term success.

TIMING – SECTION C

The PouchPlan automates much of this section with information you have already provided. Many people still find this section to be the most conceptually challenging as there are a lot of moving parts. You will find it very helpful to refer to the "Sample" tab for examples of how to accommodate your specific plan. I'm going to refer to these examples that you can use as the basis for completing the entire section.

Sections C-1 and C-2 are where we make sure you have enough money in your bank account to pay your bills as they come due. We fund the bank first, then the cash pouch. The total amount of your bills due each pay period is displayed on row 45 for your 1st paycheck and on row 58 for your 2nd paycheck. Row 63 displays the amount required to be deposited into your bank by pay period. (See Figure 11-17.)

If you have "Other Income" in section A, the next two paragraphs are for you. If you do not have any other income, you can skip this and the next paragraph. ***Other Income is manually inputted based on when it is received, how it is received, and when it is needed to fund a bank account.*** You will use row 64 to account for this income. For example, = "Child Support" of $250 is directly deposited into your bank on the 5th of the month. We enter the $250 in the first pay period on check #1. (See Figure 11-18.) We've found it best to enter the income exactly when it comes in, and then use other options on the spreadsheet to move it around if necessary. We will cover those movements in a few minutes.

11-17: Bank Deposits Required Per Paycheck

The PouchPlan spreadsheet automatically groups weeks of the month to match the timing of your income and expenses. The above example combines expenses due over multiple periods to be paid by each paycheck. This combined amount becomes the deposit required into your checking account in order to cover these expenses until your next paycheck.

	A	B	C	D	E	F	G	H	I	J	K	L	M
26	Section B-2				Check # 1	Section B - 3							
27	Regular in frequency & amount					Week of the month							
28	Spent from Checking			Comment	1st-7th	8th-15th	16th-23rd	24th-31st	5TH CK	3RD CK		CHECK	
29	Paid from Checking # 1		Amount		Amount	Amount	Amount	Amount	Amount	Amount	Total	OK	
30	Mortgage/Rent		800	Prepay 1/2	400		400				800	0	
31	Tithe		650			300		300		300	650	0	
32	Car Payment		250		200		50				250	0	
33	House Insurance		150	semiannual						900	150	0	
34	Life Insurance		25	semiannual						150	25	0	
35	Cable		80				80				80	0	
36	Internet		50	semiannual						300	50	0	
37	Electricty		200		200						200	0	
43											-	0	
44	Other										-	0	
45	Total		2,205		800	300	530	300	-	1,650	3,855	0	
59													
60		Section C-1						Section C-2					
61	DEPOSITS		Pay of #1	Pay of #1	Pay of #1	Pay of #1	Pay of #1	Pay of #2	Pay of #2	Pay of #2	Pay of #2	Pay of #2	Check
62	to Bank		1st-7th	8th-15th	16th-23rd	24th-31st	5TH/3RD	1st-7th	8th-15th	16th-23rd	24th-31st	5TH/3RD	
63	Deposit Required		1,100	-	830	-	1,650	150	90	60	180	100	
64	Other		250							0			
65	Transfers		-100	0	-90	0	0	100	0	0	80	0	0.00
66	Cash to POUCH		805	0	845	0	105	50	10	40	0	0	
67	CHECK		OK	OK	OK	OK	OK	OK	OK	OK	OK	OK	

11-18: Manual Entry of Other Income

Enter your other income as a deposit to your bank account during the week of the month it is received.

	A	B	C	D
5		Section A		
6	Pay Period	Biweekly	Weekly	Monthly
7	Checking Acct	1	2	Other
8	Pay or Income	3,000.00	100.00	250.00
9	Deductions			
10	Income Tax	300.00	-	
59				
60		Section C-1		
61	DEPOSITS		Pay of #1	Pay of #1
62	to Bank		1st-7th	8th-15th
63	Deposit Required		1,100	-
64	Other		250	
65	Transfers		-100	0
66	Cash to POUCH		805	0
67	CHECK		OK	OK

There is at least one other situation that presents a challenge to properly track. This occurs when you receive benefits on a debit card. Since the card is often restricted to certain qualifying purchases, you can't just draw cash to fund the pouch. But at the same time, we can't put it in the bank because it is never deposited. You are going to use the best option and mix the treatment of debit card benefits. You should have already entered the income amount in section A, so go to section D, at the bottom of the spreadsheet. Row 82 is labeled, "Debit Card." Decide which of the irregular expenses

11-19: Debit or EBT Card as Other Income

EBT or debit card income will be moved directly to the pouch in Section D.

	A	B	C	D	E
1	The Pouch				
2	Personal Budget Plan with Cash Timing				
3	mwalker@PouchPlan.com				
4					
5		Section A			
6	Pay Period	Biweekly	Weekly	Monthly	Monthly
7	Checking Acct	1	2	Other	Other
8	Pay or Income	3,000.00	100.00	250.00	150.00
9	Deductions				
10	Income Tax	300.00	-		
11	SS	180.00			
68					
69		Section D			
70	CASH	FOOD & HOUSE	GAS	MISC	CLOTHES
71	BREAKOUTS	750	260	253	210
72	#1 ck week #1	300	100	100	75
73	#1 ck week #2				
74	#1 ck week #3	300	160	135	100
75	#1 ck week #4				
76	#2 ck week #1			18	17
77	#2 ck week #2				
78	#2 ck week #3				
79	#2 ck week #4				
80	5th Paychecks				105
81	3rd Paychecks				
82	Debit Card	150			
83	OK = 0, +/- 3	0	0	0	0

you will assign the card to pay, then enter the amount of the card in the column based on the descriptions on row 70. The card will be put in the corresponding pouch section and used like cash when you purchase items from that category. (See Figure 11-19.)

OK, we've got everyone back on board and we are still in section C. On row 67 is a "CHECK" function that we will use to make sure we have enough funds in our account(s) to cover our expenses. If all the cells on row 67 display "OK," you are good to go and nothing else is required on your part. (See Figure 11-20.) The PouchPlan has automatically allocated your deposits and cash funding of your pouch. However, you should continue to pay attention to this part of the instructions as this situation could change later as you make adjustments to your plan, and you will need to know how to handle this issue. If one or more of the cells display "Error," we will have to move around funds or expenses to achieve an "OK" in that cell. (See Figure 11-21.) Funds are typically easiest to move, but if you have only one income, you will have to adjust

11-20: Double Checking Bank Deposits

The PouchPlan spreadsheet ensures that the deposits going into your bank are sufficient to fund your regular expenses. Line 67 will display an error message rather than "OK" if the deposits are not sufficient.

	A	B	C	D	E	F	G
60		Section C-1					
61	DEPOSITS		Pay of #1	Pay of #1	Pay of #1	Pay of #1	Pay of #1
62	to Bank		1st-7th	8th-15th	16th-23rd	24th-31st	5TH/3RD
63	Deposit Required		1,100	-	830	-	1,650
64	Other		250				
65	Transfers		-100	0	-80	0	0
66	Cash to POUCH		805	0	845	0	105
67	CHECK		OK	OK	OK	OK	OK
68							

11-21: Insufficient Deposit Error Message Displayed

The spreadsheet shows two periods where not enough money has been left in the bank account to cover regular expenses. These two errors must be corrected by either moving expenses or using transfers.

	A	B	C	D	E	F	G	H	I	J	K	L	M
58	Total		513		150	90	60	180	100	0	513	0	
59													
60		Section C-1						Section C-2					
61	DEPOSITS		Pay of #1	Pay of #1	Pay of #1	Pay of #1	Pay of #1	Pay of #2	Pay of #2	Pay of #2	Pay of #2	Pay of #2	Check
62	to Bank		1st-7th	8th-15th	16th-23rd	24th-31st	5TH/3RD	1st-7th	8th-15th	16th-23rd	24th-31st	5TH/3RD	
63	Deposit Required		1,100	-	830	-	1,660	150	90	60	180	100	
64	Other		250							0			
65	Transfers			0		0	0		0	0		0	0.00
66	Cash to POUCH		905	0	925	0	105	50	10	40	80	0	
67	CHECK		OK	OK	OK	OK	OK	ERROR	OK	OK	ERROR	OK	

the timing of your expenses. Let's look at moving funds first.

The technique you are going to use will work if you have two or more paychecks going into one account or if you use separate checking accounts for each paycheck. On row 65 (labeled "Transfers"), we are going to enter the amount we want to transfer as both a positive and a negative number. (See Figure 11-22.) The positive number is entered into the column of the account (or paycheck) you need to fund, and the negative number is entered into the column of the account from which the money is to be taken. Care needs to be taken to make sure the two amounts are entered into the correct time period for each transfer. You can always transfer the money out of an account

11-22: Transferring Money Between Accounts or Paychecks

Using transfers between accounts or paychecks to correct insufficient funds deposited to an account.

	A	B	C	D	E	F	G	H	I	J	K	L	M
58	Total		513		150	90	60	180	100	0	513	0	
59													
60		Section C-1						Section C-2					
61	DEPOSITS		Pay of #1	Pay of #1	Pay of #1	Pay of #1	Pay of #1	Pay of #2	Pay of #2	Pay of #2	Pay of #2	Pay of #2	Check
62	to Bank		1st-7th	8th-15th	16th-23rd	24th-31st	5TH/3RD	1st-7th	8th-15th	16th-23rd	24th-31st	5TH/3RD	
63	Deposit Required		1,100	-	830	-	1,660	150	90	60	180	100	
64	Other		250							0			
65	Transfers		-100	0	-80	0	0	100	0	0	80	0	0.00
66	Cash to POUCH		805	0	845	0	105	50	10	40	0	0	
67	CHECK		OK	OK	OK	OK	OK	OK	OK	OK	OK	OK	

earlier than needed. The 5th/3rd periods are not used for the transferring of funds because of timing issues.

The spreadsheet tells us the amount available for transfers by looking at row 66, which is labeled "Cash to POUCH." You can move as much as necessary as long as it is not more than the amount displayed in the period column on row 66. You can also transfer from a period that has a paycheck into a future period for another paycheck. You can't transfer from a later period to an earlier period as the cash will not be available for the transfer. If you are using only one account, the funds obviously cannot transfer back and forth. It is still a good idea to use this section to keep the two paychecks separate for the expenses they are responsible for funding. It will also alert you if one paycheck changes and results in a lack of funds required during a pay period.

For example, = column H, the 1-7th date range of paycheck/account #2 has $150 in expenses and only $100 of net pay available. You need to make sure you have at least $150 deposited into the bank in order to pay the regular expenses scheduled to come out of that check for that time frame. I'm going to show moving $100, not just the $50 needed. On the spreadsheet, go to cell H65 and enter a positive $100, moving the money into this period. Staying on row 65, go to column C (matches the same time period, but for a different paycheck/account) and enter the same $100 amount as a negative, representing the amount being taken out of the account. On the "Sample" tab worksheet, a similar situation is displayed on the 16th-23rd paycheck, but the $80 is moved forward to a later period, the 24th-31st, which is permissible. (See Figure 11-22 above.)

Sometimes, it may be necessary, or just easier, to move expenses to make sure the funds are available after each paycheck. You can always shift an expense, or part of an expense, to an earlier period and the spreadsheet will work properly. This is the easiest tactic and the one recommended. If the expense is during the first pay period of the month, you will have to "prefund" it during the latter part of the previous month. This is not as hard as it sounds. The PouchPlan is continuously up-to-date on a "rolling basis." You might end the month with $500 in your rent pouch as your rent is due on the 1st and your first paycheck is not until the 8th. Next month's rent will then be "prefunded" during the current month. A second option is to split the payment of the expense between paychecks. This is more difficult to master and is not recommended while you are new to the PouchPlan. As you gain experience and use this book, there are many advanced tactics that are available and will make sense based on your personal experience and familiarity with the spreadsheet as a tool. No matter which tactic you use, you must have row 67 display all "OKs" under each pay period.

Hopefully, it took you longer to read the last couple of instructions that it did to follow them! You only have one section left, section D.

FILLING THE POUCH – SECTION D

This is the section when you actually put your cash in your pouch. You might ask, "What exactly is this 'pouch'?" The pouch is a coupon-sized expandable file that has eight to ten sections. These are commonly available at the "mart" stores and most office supply retailers, and I offer several different pouches at www.pouchplan.com. You are going to label the sections of the pouch to match the descriptions from part B-1 of the spreadsheet. Section D will allow you to fund each category based on your hierarchy of needs combined with the available cash from each paycheck. You end up with a sheet that tells you how much cash goes into each pouch section from each paycheck. You simply withdraw cash from your bank, fund each section of the pouch per this sheet, and you are done with all your budgeting requirements until next payday. Yes, you read that right. You've spent less than five minutes, and you are done budgeting!

The PouchPlan has already filled in the description and amounts on rows 70 and 71 from your input into section B-1, your "Irregular Expenses." (You have also already entered an amount on row 82 if you had income received on a debit card.) You are going to enter amounts down each column from each paycheck until the amount displayed on row 83 is a "0." There is also a number displayed at the end of each row in column M that shows how much of each paycheck is left to allocate. You have to allocate the cash based on both what is available each pay period ("Total" in column M) and what is budgeted for expenses ("Total" on row 83). These "count down" from a number toward "0" as you apply the cash available. (See Figures 11-23.1 and 11-23.2)

How do you decide when and how much money to put in each category each time? You use your personal

11-23.1: Filling Up Your Pouch- Part 1

The example shows the cash from one paycheck being distributed to your pouch categories. Line 72 shows that distribution and, very importantly, in Column M shows check as "0". This means you have distributed all the cash from that paycheck successfully. Column M must show a "0" to indicate that you have successfully distributed the cash among your categories. There are other amounts being displayed below this in Column M because that cash has not yet been distributed. Line 83 shows the remaining funding needs of each category. The PouchPlan spreadsheet will automatically adjust these numbers as you distribute cash from other paychecks. This row must also show all "0"s when all cash has been distributed.

	A	B	C	D	E	F	G	H	I	J	K	L	M
1	The Pouch												
68													
69		Section D											
70	CASH	FOOD & HOUSE	GAS	MISC	CLOTHES	ENTRTNMNT	CAR MAINT	HAIR	GIFTS	SCHOOL	TRAVEL	Total	Check
71	BREAKOUTS	750	260	253	210	200	60	40	50	60	35	1,918	0
72	#1 ck week #1	300	100	100	75	100	40	20	40	10	20	805	0
73	#1 ck week #2											0	0
74	#1 ck week #3											0	845
75	#1 ck week #4											0	0
76	#2 ck week #1											0	50
77	#2 ck week #2											0	10
78	#2 ck week #3											0	40
79	#2 ck week #4											0	0
80	5th Paychecks											0	105
81	3rd Paychecks											0	0
82	Debit Card	$150.00										150	
83	OK = 0, +/- 3	-300	-160	-153	-135	-100	-20	-20	-10	-50	-15		1050
84													

hierarchy of needs. Food should obviously be high on everyone's list. I would think gas might be next if you have to drive to get to your job. Consider the timing of how you spend a particular expense. Food expenses are usually spread fairly evenly during the month, but you may want to allocate a bit extra early in the month as you can stock up on nonperishables to save time and money. Another gauge might be what you can easily put off until another part of the month. Sometimes, you may just have to go with your best guess and see how that works. It is very easy to change this part of the plan without affecting any other parts.

What if you don't get it right the first time? Don't worry too much about that; you will never get it

11-23.2: Filling Up Your Pouch- Part 2

The PouchPlan spreadsheet shows a successful distribution of your cash to your pouch categories. Column M and Line 83 display all "0"s showing a fully funded pouch.

	A	B	C	D	E	F	G	H	I	J	K	L	M
68													
69		Section D											
70	CASH	FOOD & HOUSE	GAS	MISC	CLOTHES	ENTRTNMNT	CAR MAINT	HAIR	GIFTS	SCHOOL	TRAVEL	Total	Check
71	BREAKOUTS	750	260	253	210	200	60	40	50	60	35	1,918	0
72	#1 ck week #1	300	100	100	75	100	40	20	40	10	20	805	0
73	#1 ck week #2											0	0
74	#1 ck week #3	300	160	135	100	35	20	20	10	50	15	845	0
75	#1 ck week #4											0	0
76	#2 ck week #1			18	17	15						50	0
77	#2 ck week #2					10						10	0
78	#2 ck week #3					40						40	0
79	#2 ck week #4											0	0
80	5th Paychecks				105							105	0
81	3rd Paychecks											0	0
82	Debit Card	150										150	
83	OK = 0, +/- 3	0	0	0	0	0	0	0	0	0	0		0
84													

perfect. The PouchPlan is always in balance, and if you have to adjust on the fly, just take from one cash category to fund another. You'll find you've had to put off your haircut or movie night or that new blouse you are dying to have, but you will be able to send a gift with your child to their friend's thirteenth birthday party!

A couple of hints that may help you as you fill in section D: Start by putting $100 in the first expense cell and watch what happens to column M and row 83. Take the same cell back to zero and notice the change in both areas again. Now go more toward the middle of the sheet and repeat this exercise. Doing this a couple of times seems to build a baseline understanding of what is happening as you fill in the matrix.

The second helpful hint is when you have changes to your section B-1 "Irregular Expenses," you will have to correct this section D as well. I find it easier to just clear out all the data and start over with each expense category rather than trying to adjust some and not the others. **Be sure and print or save a copy before you erase the current data as most of the amounts**

will not require any changes. Remember to save the spreadsheet each time you make any changes. Refer to the introduction section of this book for the best options for naming each version.

PRINTING

The spreadsheet is set to print on two pages. The first page has all the plan information, and the second has the deposit and cash breakouts. My wife liked to have only the deposit and cash breakout sheet in the pouch, and I can certainly see how having the "go to" piece of information necessary to implement the plan each payday is critical. You can, of course, change the print parameters if you so desire. This will also allow you to keep your financial information away from any wandering eyes of clerical or bank personnel.

A quick, last word. Most of the spreadsheet is locked and not available. This is not to keep you from understanding what the spreadsheet is doing, but to prevent users from accidentally overwriting a formula or informational cell that is required for the spreadsheet to function correctly. If you want to make changes, just e-mail me and I will let you have the unlock code for the area you would like to customize. The spreadsheet template is copyrighted, but all purchasers are entitled to make multiple copies for their personal use.

I WANT TO HEAR FROM YOU. My hope is to provide a workable, doable, financial foundation for all those people who have found money an area of life that seems clouded in mystery or challenging to control. Please send me your comments, criticisms, suggestions, and experiences from dealing with the

PouchPlan spreadsheet. www.pouchplan.com has a member page and blog, but also feel free to contact me at mwalker@pouchplan.com.

ACKNOWLEDGMENTS

I've been looking forward to these acknowledgments before I even wrote the first page of this book. I love saying thanks to people, especially those whose gifts of time and effort have made a difference in my life. I realize that most readers will not pay much attention to this section. I am guilty of the very same omission in most of the books I've read. I feel a little bad about that now, because I have a much clearer picture of how many people's influence and participation are necessary to bring a book to print.

Let me start first with the professional staff that took my wandering ideas and tangent thoughts and forced them into a cohesive book. My editor Madalyn Stone provided timely and sage thoughts and direction. She made me sound like a writer. Jerry Dorris handled the outside and inside layout and design. I think the only feedback I ever gave him was "that looks great!"

Steve and Bill Harrison's Quantum Leap program was the umbrella under which I sheltered to gain the protection of experts as I became an author. Quality people with a quality program. Within Quantum Leap were talented coaches and advisors to whom I turned for their skilled direction. To Geoffrey Berwind, Brian Edmondson, Deb Englander, Mary Giuseffi and Gail Snyder, your expertise and guidance allowed me to move through an unfamiliar territory as though it was my backyard. I owe a special debt of gratitude to Martha Bullen, my main book coach. From friendly encouragement to hard deadlines, you kept me focused on what was next and on what was important. Thanks to all of you.

Four men have influenced me tremendously. Charles Wright was my football and track coach for six years. He taught me that while winning was important, it was not everything. What you became during the competition was much more important. Art Scharlach was my tennis partner, banker and friend; he was good at all three and was never afraid to stand with me no matter the situation. He showed me the difference between a friend and an acquaintance. Brent Williams spent nearly 3 years meeting with me at 6am on Wednesday mornings. He showed me how faith put into action will literally move mountains. Bill Means is my brother in law, but also much more. Always interested and supportive of me, he has been a true sounding board whose life experience gave him wisdom. He shared that wisdom and his friendship with me through thick and thin times. These men taught me life's truths. I have been able to pass these truths on to my children and grandchildren because of their investment in me. That's a special kind of compounding interest!

In my professional career, I have been fortunate to have coworkers with competence, class and character. Chief among them were Craig Rutledge, Les McElveen, and James Blevins. There were many others, but I saw these men do the right thing over and over each day under tremendous pressures. I also had some really good bosses over the years. Roy Henry and Gary Gagnon were at the top of that list. Their leadership opened many doors for me that I could not have opened on my own.

My siblings, Mollie, Clayton, Ashley and Kirby have consistently shared my delight or disappointment no matter what trek I was on. And I've been on plenty. My children, Mathew, Erin Dell, Leslie (special thanks for all the editing!), Christopher and Leigh Anne have actually lived through what I've written about. I've made many mistakes I'm sure, but I hope you find in these pages some truths that illuminate my love for each of you. You each have strengths that are amazing. I am among the most blessed of all men because of you. My wife and co-creator of the PouchPlan, Suzanne, is simply amazing. Thank you for your support and sacrifice while I wrote this book. Thank you for your support, sacrifice and love while we lived it! I could not have done either without you.